THE

GOETIA

Figure 1. *Self-portrait of Aleister Crowley as Frater Perdurabo evoking the spirit Paimon to visible appearance.*

THE

GOETIA

THE LESSER KEY OF
SOLOMON THE KING

LEMEGETON, BOOK I
CLAVICULA SALOMONIS REGIS

TRANSLATED BY

SAMUEL LIDDELL
MACGREGOR MATHERS

EDITED, ANNOTATED, INTRODUCED AND ENLARGED BY

ALEISTER CROWLEY

ILLUSTRATED SECOND EDITION WITH NEW ANNOTATIONS BY

ALEISTER CROWLEY

EDITED BY

HYMENAEUS BETA

ⓦ **WEISERBOOKS**
San Francisco, CA / Newburyport, MA

First published in 1995 by
Red Wheel/Weiser, LLC
500 Third Street, Suite 230
San Francisco, CA 94107
www.redwheelweiser.com

Revised and corrected second printing, 1997

ISBN: 978-0-87728-847-3

Library of Congress Cataloging-in-Publication Data:

Clavicula Salomonis. English.
    The Goetia : the lesser key of Solomon the King : Lemegeton—Clavicula Salomonis Regis, book one / translated by Samuel Liddell MacGregor Mathers: edited, annotated, and introduced with addition by Aleister Crowley : illustrated second edition with new annotations by Aleister Crowley : edited by Hymenaeus Beta.
        p.   cm.
    ISBN 087728-847-X
    1. Magic. I. Mathers, S. L. MacGregor (Samuel Liddell MacGregor), 1854-1918, II. Crowley, Aleister, 1875-1947. III. Hymenaeus Beta. IV. Title
    BF1611.C5413   1995
    133.4'3—dc20   95-37057
                                                                              CIP

Illustrations of Goëtic demons on the cover by Louis Breton from Collin de Plancy's *Dictionnaire Infernal*, 6th edition (1863).
Cover and book design by Spirit Vision, Inc.
Typeset in 12 point Sabon

Printed in Canada
TCP
12 11 10 9 8

The paper used in this publication meets the minimum requirements of the American National Standard for Information Sciences—Permanence of Paper for Printed Library Materials Z39.48-1992(R1997).

Table of Contents

Table of Figures

Abbreviations and Editorial Conventions

G.D.   Hermetic Order of the Golden Dawn

E.V.   *era vulgari* or "in the common era"

ED.   Editor (Aleister Crowley)

TRANS. Translator (S. L. Mathers)

[ ]   Editorial notes and insertions by the present editor. In footnotes, these brackets distinguish editorial notes from those by Crowley or Mathers.

{ }   Editorial notes by Crowley that appeared in brackets [ ] in the first edition.

< >   Manuscript notes transferred to a copy of the *Goetia* by G.J. Yorke from Crowley's MS. notes in a second copy.

( )   Manuscript notes and textual changes in Crowley's hand in his vellum copy of the *Goetia*.

⌐ ¬   Corrected reading in the Preliminary Invocation, relying on the Greek transcription text of Goodwin.

⟦ ⟧   Restored lacuna in the Preliminary Invocation, relying on the Greek transcription text of Goodwin.

Figure 2. King Solomon evoking Belial.
From Jacobus de Teramo, Hie hebt sich an das Buch Belial genant *(Augsburg, 1473).*

Editor's Foreword

to the Second Edition

"LITTLE BROTHER, you have been meddling with the *Goetia*!"

These were the first words of Allan Bennett MacGregor (Frater Iehi Aour, 1872–1923) to Aleister Crowley (Frater Perdurabo, 1875–1947). It was early in 1899, and the occasion was a ceremony at the Isis-Urania Temple of the Hermetic Order of the Golden Dawn (hereinafter the G.D.) in London.[1] It was not quite their first meeting; Crowley had been, as he put it, "led trembling before the great man" only an hour earlier, but found himself dumbstruck. Crowley timidly denied Bennett's charge, modestly declaring himself "unworthy even to pronounce the word," to which Bennett replied, "in that case the *Goetia* has been meddling with you."[2]

What is remarkable about this exchange is that the fearsome Bennett was only a few years Crowley's senior—both were in their twenties—and had become a G.D. Neophyte in 1894,[3] just four years before Crowley. That Bennett should inspire such awe is perhaps more understandable if one considers that he was the adoptive son and protégé of the G.D.'s leader, Samuel Liddell MacGregor Mathers (1854–1918).[4]

---

[1] Possibly Crowley's own 2°=9° initiation that January. See Crowley's chronology in ΘΕΛΗΜΑ, *The Holy Books of Thelema* (*Equinox* III(9), York Beach, ME: Weiser, 1983, 1990), p. xvi. Elsewhere Crowley mentions their first meeting as occurring in the spring.

[2] This account of their meeting relies on two sources, Crowley's "The Revival of Magick," *The International* XI(8–11), Aug.–Nov. 1917 (a reprint is in press), and *The Confessions of Aleister Crowley*, abridged ed., ed. John Symonds and Kenneth Grant (London: Cape, 1969; rpt. London and New York: Arkana, 1989), p. 178 (cited hereinafter as *Confessions*). Perhaps Bennett's barb hit home because Crowley's first book on magic, A.E. Waite's *The Book of Black Magic and of Pacts* (London: Redway, 1898), contains a synopsis of the *Goetia*.

[3] This is based on the date Bennett received his Neophyte documents (December 12, 1894); these papers survive in transcripts made by J.F.C. Fuller.

[4] Like Mathers, Bennett at times used the Scottish clan name MacGregor. O.H. de A. Wijesekera writes that "his father died early and he was adopted by S.L. MacGregor, the Head of a society called the Hermetic Order of the Golden Dawn" in his foreword to Ananda Metteyya [Allan Bennett], *Culture of Mind* (Colombo: Bauddha Sahitya Sabha, 1945), p. i.

Bennett took Crowley as his magical student, moving into Crowley's flat where he undertook to teach Crowley everything he knew about magic. This arrangement lasted less than a year, as Bennett suffered from life-threatening asthma and needed to leave England for a warmer climate where he hoped to study Eastern philosophy.

Curiously, just as the Goetia had provided the pretext for Bennett's first overture to Crowley, it provided the means for his leave-taking. Crowley was wealthy and Bennett penniless. Crowley could easily have paid Bennett's passage from England, but was sensitive to even the appearance of paying for spiritual instruction, and thus sought to help by indirect means. Crowley and George Cecil Jones evoked the Goëtic spirit Buer, whose particular speciality is healing. They succeeded in materializing Buer to where he appeared to the physical sight, but the form did not match the description in the Goetia so they considered the operation a failure. But as Crowley later recounted, "'miraculous' things began to happen; in one way and another the gates opened for Allan to migrate to less asthmatic climes; and the object of our work was amply attained."[5] Bennett left England for Ceylon in January 1900, leaving his magical manuscripts with Crowley. He became a Buddhist monk in 1902.

S. L. Mathers was not a particularly original thinker, but had a genius for correlating his researches in the libraries of England and France into a coherent system, and this synthesis is the essential G.D. legacy today. He published several magical and qabalistic works, including the first English edition of a portion of the Zohar entitled The Kabbalah Unveiled,[6] and an edition of the greater Key of Solomon.[7] By 1899 he was at work on an edition of the Lemegeton (of which the Goetia is part) commissioned by Crowley,[8] and The Sacred Magic of Abra-Melin the Mage.[9]

According to its own foundation story, the Hermetic Order of the Golden Dawn owed its existence to the chance discovery of documents written in cipher found in a London bookstall. Once deciphered, they gave the outlines of an initiatic system and an address in Germany for a Soror Sapiens Dominabitur Astris or Fraülein Sprengel, who replied to an inquiry with permission to establish a branch of the Order outlined in the documents, supposedly a survival of the legendary Rosicrucian Fraternity.[10]

---

[5] Aleister Crowley, "Beings I have Seen with my Physical Eye," Magick without Tears, letter 57 (unabridged edition, ed. Karl J. Germer, Hampton, NJ: Thelema, 1954; abridged ed., ed. Israel Regardie, rpt. Scottsdale, AZ: New Falcon, 1991).

[6] S. L. Mathers, ed. and trans., The Kabbalah Unveiled (London: Kegan Paul, Trench and Trubner, 1887; rpt. York Beach, ME: Weiser, 1993).

[7] S. L. Mathers, ed. and trans., The Key of Solomon the King (London: Redway, 1889; rpt. York Beach, ME: Weiser, 1972, 1992).

[8] See Crowley's statement to this effect, quoted on page xvii.

[9] S. L. Mathers, ed. and trans., The Book of the Sacred Magic of Abra-Melin the Mage (London: Watkins, 1900; rpt. New York: Dover, 1975).

[10] See Ellic Howe, The Magicians of the Golden Dawn (London: Routledge and Kegan Paul, 1972; rpt. New York: Weiser, 1978) and R.A. Gilbert's The Golden Dawn: Twilight of the Magicians (Wellingborough: Aquarian, 1983); Gilbert has produced the best recent scholarship on the subject in various articles. For the Gold- und Rosenkreuz, the 18th century German neo-Rosicrucian order with structural similarities to the S.R.I.A. and the G.D., see Christopher McIntosh, The Rose Cross and the Age of Reason (Leiden and New York: Brill, 1992). For the background of the late 19th century occult renaissance in England see Joscelyn Godwin, The Theosophical Enlightenment (Albany, NY: SUNY Press, 1995).

The founders were Dr. W. Wynn Westcott, Dr. W.R. Woodman and S.L. Mathers, all active in English esoteric and masonic circles, particularly the Societas Rosicruciana in Anglia (S.R.I.A.).[11] The G.D. flourished after its foundation in 1887–88, attracting the active participation of members like the poets W.B. Yeats and A.E. Waite. With the death of Woodman and the resignation of Westcott, only Mathers remained of the founders, and he governed as Chief Adept of the Order from Paris.

The Golden Dawn was the outermost of three orders. The Second Order was the R.R. et A.C. (Rosæ Rubeæ et Aureæ Crucis—the Rose of Ruby and the Cross of Gold, a name with intentional Rosicrucian overtones), and there was a Third Order with its præterhuman "Secret Chiefs," who governed the lower orders through select intermediaries, and from whom the spiritual teachings ultimately derived.

Crowley's introducer to the G.D. was George Cecil Jones (Frater Volo Noscere). After Bennett's departure for the East, he was Crowley's closest magical colleague. After his first initiation in November of 1898, Crowley advanced through the remaining grades of the G.D. in only six months. Admission to the Second Order, the R.R. et A.C., was invitational, and the decision rested solely with Mathers in Paris, whom Crowley first met in May of 1899. Crowley was soon invited (the recommendations of Bennett and Jones may be presumed), and took his 5°=6° initiation in Paris in January of 1900.

Many G.D. members in London had come to distrust the usually absent Mathers, and question his authority. His new favorite Crowley became the object of rumor and gossip (the bane of occult societies then as now) about his "doubtful" character. That resentment of Mathers should be transferred to Crowley is understandable. Even Ithell Colquhoun, author of a biographical study of Mathers that is notably unsympathetic to Crowley, described him as Mathers' heir-apparent.[12] Some London members opposed Crowley's Second Order initiation for fear that Mathers would put him in charge in London; others probably didn't think him "clubbable."

After Crowley's Second Order initiation he returned to London and requested his official grade papers from the London Second Order. In open defiance of order procedure and Mathers' wishes, he was refused. The London Temple was in revolt.

Mathers claimed to have established direct contact with the invisible Secret Chiefs. Apparently concerned that London members might turn to Westcott for leadership he sought to undermine his credibility, writing to a London Second Order member that Westcott had

> NEVER been at *any time* either in personal or written communication with the Secret
> Chiefs of the Order, he having *either himself forged* or *procured to be forged* the
> professed correspondence between him and them, and my tongue having been tied

---

[11] These close historical ties between the S.R.I.A. and the Golden Dawn were long obscured. Golden Dawn temples deriving from the original Order still exist in Paris and London; the latter is reportedly closely affiliated to the S.R.I.A. Mathers renamed his branch the Hermetic Order of A∴O∴ (Alpha and Omega); it was conducted by his wife Moina after his death. The American branch, headquartered in Philadelphia, went inactive in the 1930s; its papers are now in the O.T.O. Archives.

[12] Ithell Colquhoun, *Sword of Wisdom: MacGregor Mathers and the Golden Dawn* (New York: Putnam's, 1975), p. 91.

all these years by a Previous Oath of Secrecy to him, demanded by him, from me, before showing me what he had either done or caused to be done or both.[13]

This backfired, spreading quickly through the British membership and provoking a crisis of confidence in the initiatory *bona fides* of the Order, and casting further doubt on the Third Order, its Secret Chiefs, and their representative Mathers.[14]

Crowley was by this time at home in Scotland, preparing to undertake the rigorous Abra-Melin operation to obtain the Knowledge and Conversation of the Holy Guardian Angel. When the London Second Order rebelled, he set aside his spiritual work to assist Mathers who "was my only link with the Secret Chiefs to whom I was pledged. I wrote to him offering to place myself and my fortune unreservedly at his disposal; if that meant giving up the Abra-Melin Operation for the present, all right." He went to Paris and made various proposals for the reform of the London Second Order and for resolving the crisis.[15]

Crowley travelled to London as Mathers' personal envoy, charged with obtaining oaths of loyalty from the rebellious brethren and securing the temple properties. Crowley appeared masked, in full Highland regalia,[16] but it was yet another defeat for the Scots cause, this time at the hands of a King's Counsel retained by a London Second Order member, Annie Horniman. The foray was not a complete loss; according to J.F.C. Fuller, Crowley succeeded in recovering the uncompleted manuscript of Mathers' edition of the *Lemegeton*, which would become the present book.[17] The Second Order in London, without clear leadership, retired to committee and never emerged.[18] It later spawned several derivative groups.

Crowley was intensely loyal, but adamant against those who proved unworthy in his eyes, which he took almost as a personal betrayal. He began to have doubts about Mathers, suspecting that his work on *The Sacred Magic of Abra-Melin* had undone him spiritually, and became inactive as an Order member until he could discuss his dilemma with Allan Bennett, which he did in Burma in 1902. He returned to England disillusioned with Mathers as Chief Adept, but not with the Order itself.

Crowley must have been aware that Mathers viewed him as a potential successor, and as a keen student of J.G. Frazer he took steps to accelerate the succession. One

---

[13] Mathers, letter to Florence Farr Emery, Feb. 16, 1900; see Crowley, *Confessions*, p. 194.

[14] Mathers' later claim that he was working directly with Soror S.D.A. in Paris did nothing to ameliorate matters, and his credibility was shattered when it was revealed that the woman in question was an impostor—Mme. Horos—who was later (with her husband) convicted in England of serious charges that brought the Golden Dawn unfavorable publicity.

[15] *Confessions*, p. 195. Notably, the rule that "each member will know only the member who introduced him" was later applied by Crowley in the A∴ A∴.

[16] Probably wearing the MacGregor tartan since, like Mathers and Bennett, Crowley claimed a MacGregor connection. This was probably through his Grant family relations; ironically, the Grant family was recognized as the "official" MacGregor line as a reward for betraying the Scots cause after Culloden.

[17] Keith Hogg, *666: Bibliotheca Crowleyana. Catalog of a unique Collection ... formed, with an Introductory Essay, by Major-General J.F.C. Fuller* (Tenterden, Kent: Keith Hogg [1966]; rpt. Seattle: Holmes, n.d.), p. 16.

[18] In addition to Crowley's own first-hand accounts, Howe, op. cit.; Gilbert, op. cit., and George Mills Harper, *Yeats's Golden Dawn* (London: MacMillan, 1974), which gives W. B. Yeats' pamphlet "Is the R.R. et A.C. to Remain a Magical Order?" as an appendix.

of the principal weapons in his armamentarium was his edition of the *Goetia*, which appeared in 1904. Its title page declared that it had been "translated into the English tongue by a dead hand and adorned with divers other matters germane, delightful to the wise, the whole edited, verified, introduced and commented by Aleister Crowley." Crowley's editorial additions were calculated to intimidate Mathers and notify members of the old Second Order of his intentions. Crowley was a great humorist who delighted in obscure and learned allusions, and part of the fun in reading his edition of the *Goetia* is deciphering his elaborate jokes at Mathers' expense, some of which are explicated below. Crowley recounts:

> I had employed Mathers to translate[19] the text of *The Lesser Key of Solomon the King* of which the *Goetia* is the first section. He got no further; after the events of 1900, he had simply collapsed morally. I added a translation of the conjurations into the Enochian or Angelic language; edited and annotated the text, prefixed a "Preliminary Invocation,"[20] added a prefatory note,[21] a Magical Square (intended to prevent improper use of the book)[22] and ultimately an Invocation of Typhon[23] when the First Magical War of the Æon of Horus was declared.[24]

---

[19] Crowley, writing years later for his *Confessions*, persisted in referring to Mathers as the translator, but the book had not been translated "from numerous MSS. in Hebrew, Latin, French and English," as he states in his Prefatory Note, but merely transcribed from vernacular English MSS, as no Hebrew, Latin or French MSS. of the *Goetia* are known to exist. It is unlikely that Crowley knew this, as he seems to have accepted Mathers' claim to a translation credit. This dubious credit has been retained in this edition; it was given anonymously on the title page of the first edition, as translated by a "dead hand." This phrase is normally complementary — meaning a skilled individual who who can do something consistently — but in this context it seems to be a witticism directed at Mathers.

[20] As explained below, this ritual is an adaptation of a Greek exorcism rite for use as an invocation of the Holy Guardian Angel, from Charles Wycliffe Goodwin, *Fragment of a Græco-Egyptian Work upon Magic from a Papyrus in the British Museum* (Cambridge: Deighton; Macmillan; London: J.W. Parker; Oxford: J.H. Parker, 1852).

[21] The Prefatory Note is riddled with Rosicrucian allusions and assaults upon Mathers. A.G.R.C. presumably means *Ad Gloriam Rosæ Crucis* (to the glory of the Rosy Cross); the meaning of A.R.G.C. is unknown, but arrangements of these letters appear around the 5°=6° altar in the G.D. Crowley's allusion to D.D.C.F. (Mathers under his Second Order motto) having succumbed to "the assaults of the Four Great Princes" is an allusion to *Abra-Melin*, which Mathers had just published, this being the ordeal facing the aspirant after the Knowledge and Conversation of the Holy Guardian Angel. Crowley goes on to suggest that by clairvoyant means he had established that Mr. and Mrs. Mathers had been "astrally displaced" by the Horos couple (Sor. S.V.A. and Fra. H.). The reference to Mrs. Mathers as his "Hermetic Mul[ier]" or wife is an allusion to the supposedly platonic nature of their marriage. "His Bishoprick let another take" is from Acts I:20 (1611 Coverdale ed.) where it applies to Judas, rather than Mathers as Crowley uses it. The closing Latin phrase is a Rosicrucian formula, the final words of the *Book T* held by Christian Rosenkreuz in the 1614 *Fama Fraternitatis*. The "Mountain of A." is the Mount Abiegnus of Rosicrucian lore, and Corpus Christi the traditional day of the convocation of the brethren of R.C.

[22] This Abramelin square, "to undo any Magic soever," is from Mathers, trans., *Abra-Melin*, p. 190 (see note 9 for full citation). The square is given on p. 2 of the present edition.

[23] This Greek curse appears with a modern translation on p. 2 of the present edition. Dating from the 3rd century E.V., it is intended to inflict catalepsy; Crowley modified it to specify Mathers. Crowley adapted it from Goodwin, op. cit.

[24] Crowley, *Confessions*, p. 362.

This preliminary skirmish—Britain's answer to the astral battles of de Guaita and Boullan—erupted after Crowley's return to Scotland from Cairo, where he had received *The Book of the Law*. On finding that Mathers had attacked him, Crowley

> employed the appropriate talismans from *The Book of the Sacred Magic of Abra-Melin* against him, evoking Beelzebub and his forty-nine servitors. ... the magical assaults ceased.[25]

As we will see, a major battle in this war would be fought some seven years later in two of the lowest hells—the press and the courts.

1904 was also the year that Mathers received a typescript copy of *The Book of the Law* from Crowley, with its accompanying message that he had been replaced by the Secret Chiefs as Chief Adept.[26] With the *Goetia*, Crowley publicly declared himself the Chief of the Rosicrucian Fraternity, or at least the R.R. et A.C.—it is doubtful that Crowley drew any distinction at this early stage of his career. The title page to his Enochian translation of the conjurations (page 95 infra) is unambiguous, referring to "our Illustrious and ever-Glorious Frater, ye Wise Perdurabo, that Myghtye Chiefe of ye Rosy-Cross Fraternitye, now sepulchred in ye Vault of ye Collegium S.S." Crowley never openly repented this youthful excess, but he did later develop a more pragmatic and skeptical attitude to the problem of Rosicrucian derivation.

For Mathers, perhaps the most worrying item in the *Goetia* was Crowley's ominous footnote: "The true life of this man and his associates ... may be looked for in my forthcoming volume: *History of the Order of the Golden Dawn*" (see page 26 infra). Mathers promptly expelled Crowley from the G.D. in 1905 because "he had circulated libels against [Mathers] and was working against the interests of the Order."[27] It is likely that the *Goetia* was the proximate cause of his expulsion.

Around 1907 Jones and Crowley assumed the offices of Præmonstrator and Imperator of the R.R. et A.C. and G.D. orders, which they formally subsumed under the true name of the Third Order, known in the outer only by its initials, the A∴A∴. They began publishing the Order's periodical, *The Equinox*, in 1909, which included a serialization of Crowley's magical career entitled "The Temple of Solomon the King," coauthored with Capt. J.F.C. Fuller, the Cancellarius of the A∴A∴. The promised account of the G.D. and its rituals began to appear in the second number of *The Equinox*. In 1910 Mathers obtained an injunction to stop the publication of the third number, but the injunction was overturned on appeal after two days.

In the wake of Crowley's highly-publicized magical performances, *The Rites of Eleusis*, a press campaign began to "examine" the A∴A∴ and its leadership. De Wend Fenton's racing tabloid *The Looking Glass* described the A∴A∴ as "a blasphemous sect, whose proceedings conceivably lend themselves to immorality of the most revolting character,"[28] and most of the articles alluded to Crowley's notoriety and

---

[25] *Confessions*, pp. 408–409. Crowley left other suggestive material in his fiction, especially *Moonchild* (London: Mandrake, 1929; rpt. York Beach, ME: Weiser, 1992), where various G.D. members appear under other names. Mathers is "Douglas," Dr. Berridge is "Dr. Balloch," Waite is "Arthwait," and Yeats is "Gates."

[26] See the account of the reception of *The Book of the Law* in connection with Crowley's relationship with Mathers in the Editor's Introduction to *Book Four (Liber ABA, Parts I-IV)* (York Beach, ME: Weiser, 1994), pp. xxxv–xlii.

[27] "Jones v. The Looking Glass," *The Looking Glass*, May 6, 1911, p. 6.

[28] *The Looking Glass*, Oct. 29, 1910.

Figure 3.
Crowley and Mathers as they
appeared during the Jones v.
Looking Glass trial.
Captioned "Remarkable
Rosicrucian Order Libel
Action," The Daily Mirror,
April 27, 1911.

evil character. George Cecil Jones was mentioned in the context of one of these attacks as an associate of Crowley's, and Jones construed this as libel. Crowley was of course the actual target, but he declined to take legal action.[29]

Jones served *The Looking Glass* with a writ for criminal libel. The trial participants included two A∴A∴ officers, Jones as plaintiff and Capt. J.F.C. Fuller, who testified for Jones. Testifying for the defense was none other than S.L. MacGregor Mathers, joined by his new English plenipotentiary Dr. E.W. Berridge; their only reason for participating was revenge against Crowley, who was present but was not called as a witness by either side. Fuller later asked Jones why he had not subpoenaed Crowley. Jones replied "if, as my friend, he had not the decency to come forward willingly, it would have been an insult to myself had I compelled him to do so."[30]

The trial was bizarre, compared by the presiding judge in the presence of the jury to the trial in *Alice in Wonderland*—a pun on the defendant *The Looking Glass.* Under oath, Mathers cheerfully affirmed his headship of the Rosicrucian Order, but Jones, who as an officer of A∴A∴ took a more *sub rosa* stance when confronted with this question, stated simply that "honestly I do not know except from having read the Seventeenth Century Tracts whether there is or was such a society."[31]

Dr. E.W. Berridge testified about the crux of the issue, Crowley's reputation:

> *Berridge:* On one occasion when Crowley was over here as an envoy on official matters concerning the Order [probably in 1900] I had the opportunity of speaking alone to him, and I said to him: "Do you know what they accuse you of?"— meaning the members of the Order. I will not express it too plainly as I see there are ladies in the Court.
>
> *Mr. Justice Scrutton:* Any ladies who may be in this Court probably are beyond any scruples of that sort.
>
> *Berridge:* Well, I said, "They accuse you of unnatural vice," and he made a very peculiar answer; he neither admitted it nor denied it. The answer was this—I presume my answer is privileged. He said, mentioning the name of some men I do not remember, "So and so has been to my place and he stopped all night, and So and So has been to my place and he stopped all night and So and So has been to my place and he stopped all night; ladies have been to my place—I will not say they stopped all night—but the police can find out nothing about me for more than two years or eighteen months back." That was such an extraordinary statement that it has remained fixed in my mind ever since.[32]

---

[29] For Crowley's account of this trial see his *Confessions*, pp. 638–643.

[30] J.F.C. Fuller, introductory essay to Keith Hogg, op. cit., p. 8.

[31] "Jones v. The Looking Glass," *The Looking Glass*, May 6, 1911, p. 3.

[32] Op. cit., p. 7. Crowley responds in his *Confessions*, abridged ed., p. 641: "The evidence against me was ... my alleged remark in the spring of 1910 [sic, read 1900], which even if I had made it, might have meant anything or nothing in the absence of any context."

Not surprisingly, Jones lost both the case and his close relationship with Crowley. J.F.C. Fuller dropped Crowley entirely over this affair. Mathers had wanted to strike back at Crowley and the A∴A∴ for their exposure of the G.D., and succeeded in personally estranging the senior officers of the A∴A∴ from one another. Crowley believed Mathers to have become a tool of the Black Lodge, which works in opposition to the Great White Brotherhood or A∴A∴, and the loss of Jones and Fuller was undoubtedly a setback. But Crowley kept on, and the A∴A∴ thrived in the following years, given added impetus by the trial publicity. The G.D. (or as Mathers renamed it, the Hermetic Order of the Alpha and Omega) fared less well.

Why did Crowley not himself sue, or testify for Jones? Crowley gives his own explanation in his *Confessions*, but even this necessarily sidestepped the truth: Crowley was a bisexual in Edwardian England. With its hangover of Victorian sex hypocrisy and hysteria, homosexuality was a felony. Oscar Wilde had suffered his not-so-rosy crucifixion only a few years earlier; unless willing to lie under oath, Crowley did not dare take the stand. Jones and Fuller failed to grasp his predicament; they were both, as the English still say, "family men." Crowley declared himself "content to await the acquittal of history,"[33] and thanks to social evolution—changes Crowley himself predicted—we may now at last say that history has returned its verdict.

⚥   ⚥   ⚥

What is a "demon," our nearly meaningless English word that derives from what the Greeks called the *daimon*, and the Romans the *dæmon*? Crowley frequently relied on the etymology or origins of words to elucidate their real meaning. Plato derived the word from δαήμων ("knowing"), but a modern authority suggests that

> the etymology more likely stems from the root δαίω, "to divide (destinies)." Thus the word could designate one's "fate" or "destiny," or the spirit controlling one's fate, one's "genius."[34]

Some of the earliest records of "minor spirits"—that is to say, spiritual entities that were not well-established gods or goddesses—come from Sumeria and Babylonia, where they were understood to be frequently attached to, albeit quite distinct from, individual people.[35] Like ourselves, such spirits had both good and bad qualities and propensities, and were an accepted fact of everyday life.

As Anthony Burgess quipped, supernature abhors a supervacuum, and influenced by Persian dualism, the Babylonians demonized many of these spirits and consigned them to a spiritual underworld.[36] Their original import began to be obscured, and so

---

[33] Crowley, *Confessions*, p. 639.

[34] See G.J. Riley's entry for "demon" in Karel van der Toorn, Bob Becking and Pieter W. van der Horst, *Dictionary of Deities and Demons in the Bible* (Leiden and New York: Brill, 1995), p. 445.

[35] See Jeremy Black and Anthony Green, *Gods, Demons and Symbols of Ancient Mesopotamia* (London: British Museum Press and Austin: University of Texas Press, 1992).

[36] See Julian Jaynes, *The Origin of Consciousness in the Breakdown of the Bicameral Mind* (Boston: Houghton Mifflin, 1976) for a brilliant thesis that accounts for the loss of widespread individual contact with the numinous. A less academic but suggestive study is Patrick Harpur, *Daimonic Reality* (London and New York: Viking Arkana, 1994). It is useful to compare these works with Crowley's 1903 essay "The Initiated Interpretation of Ceremonial Magic," p. 15 infra, arguably the foundation text of modern magical theory.

it has remained for over two millennia. The legend of the Fall from Eden is a spiritual memory of this. Jewish and Christian theologians adopted this divide-and-conquer approach to human consciousness and separated spirits into ever more elaborate angelic and demonic hierarchies.[37] Ever since, it has taken the infrequent prophet/initiate—a Plato, Iamblichus, Blake or Crowley—to remind us of our divine birthright. Crowley went further, declaring that the evolutionary goal of the new age inaugurated by his reception of *The Book of the Law* was nothing less than the conscious attainment by each individual of the Knowledge and Conversation of their *daimon* or Holy Guardian Angel. This is, he declared, the Next Step in human evolution.

The Book of the Law's dictum "Do what thou wilt shall be the whole of the Law" admits more than might be apparent at first reading. Crowley made each individual's realization of their Holy Guardian Angel or *daimon* central to the religious, magical and social system of Thelema—itself a Greek word meaning "will." He taught that each individual possessed a *true* will which was identified with the *daimon* or Guardian Angel; to know the one is to know the other. Crowley placed the emphasis on true will rather than free will, as he sought to reconcile individual volition with fate, destiny, and that inborn spark that makes us uniquely who we are—our innate genius. Self-realization of this is, according to Crowley, the true purpose of Magick, to which all of its various branches are subordinate. Indeed, he taught that:

> the Single Supreme Ritual is the attainment of the Knowledge and Conversation of the Holy Guardian Angel. *It is the raising of the complete man in a vertical straight line.* Any deviation from this line tends to become black magic. Any other operation *is* black magic.[38]

Crowley believed that much could be learnt about one's true will indirectly, through the study of one's astrological makeup, and through yoga and meditative self-analysis. He had a particularly high regard for the Buddhist systems that classify and isolate the components of ego-consciousness. He also taught that recovering memories of previous incarnations helps one understand the karmic factors operating in one's present life. On the one hand, Crowley used the phrase "Knowledge and Conversation of the Holy Guardian Angel" as a signifier for processes that cannot be described rationally and are too personal to admit generalization. On the other hand, he took it quite literally in practice; his most frequent admonition was "invoke often!" He himself considered this the key to his own spiritual attainment.

Crowley was a spiritual pragmatist. While placing no faith in remote celestial hierarchies, he admitted the "reality" of spirits in consciousness. For a Christian, it would probably approach the height of blasphemy to use a rite for expelling demons to invoke angels, but the spiritual techniques are very nearly identical, as the attention and cooperation of the spirit is obtained in either case. Crowley's favorite ritual for invoking the Holy Guardian Angel was just such a ritual—an adaptation of a 4th

---

[37] Aspects of some forms of the Hebrew Qabalah are a product of this process, as are the hierarchies of Pseudo-Dionysus, later given literary form by Dante. For early references to infernal hierarchies see Luke 11:18, 26 and Ephesians 6:12; for exorcism of demons see Matthew 12:28. In Biblical times, to believe in a deity other than the one God was to be considered possessed. A few demon-names in the *Goetia* derive from pre-monotheistic deity names in the Bible; see *Dictionary of Deities and Demons in the Bible*, particularly the entries for Asmodeus, Astarte (Ashtoreth), Baal-Berith (Berith) and possibly Baalat (Beleth, Bilet).

[38] Crowley, *Book Four, Part III*, chap. 21.

century E.V. Græco-Egyptian gnostic papyrus of a rite of exorcism.[39] Crowley even goes so far as to suggest that one of the Goëtic conjurations might be used to summon one's Guardian Angel.[40] After all, even Jacob wrestled with an angel, and would not let go unless blessed (Genesis 32:26).

Astrological spiritism has long been intertwined with questions of fate, destiny and human character, and celestial influences evolved distinct personalities. Plato called the fixed stars and planets divine and eternal animals, and Aristotle considered them præterhuman intelligences and visible deities. Astrological influences and the spirits that personified them provided an observational framework and vocabulary for making sense of life's lesser mysteries, such as why some individuals prosper and others do not. The essence of the magical method was and is to learn these secrets of nature, their modes of influence, names and associated images, and as it were turn the tables on nature, compelling its assistance by magical means. As far back as Babylonia, most demons were a mixture of human and animal, or purely theriomorphic, as they are still.[41] This is nowhere better illustrated than in the *Goetia*, which is basically a catalogue of astrological spirits.

Goetia derives from the Greek word for sorcery or witchcraft (γοητεία), and a related word γοήτης means "a wailer" (closer to Crowley's etymology, "howling"), suggestive of the "barbarous names of evocation" referred to in *The Chaldæan Oracles*, which exhorts the magician to "never change barbarous names."[42]

---

[39] "The Preliminary Invocation," first published as such in the 1904 *Goetia*, was derived from the London Papyrus 46 published in Goodwin, pp. 6–9 (see note 20 for citation). Crowley refers to it as "The Ritual of the Heart girt with a Serpent" in *Liber CXI vel Aleph* (2nd ed. York Beach, ME: Weiser, 1991), p. 108, and it is also well-known as "The Bornless Ritual"; all three titles are given in this edition, where it appears on p. 5 infra. I have not found any manuscripts of this ritual in early G.D. papers, and it is not a part of the advanced 5°=6° Theoricus curriculum. The evidence suggests that Allan Bennett was the author of this recension. He adapted part of the Goodwin translation in his "Ritual for the Evocation unto Visible Appearance of ... Taphthartharath," a ritual performed in 1896 and published in "The Temple of Solomon the King," *The Equinox* I(3) (1910), p. 178. Only the rubric is used, but the wording is essentially that of the *Goetia* version, including the interpolation of additional text not in Goodwin. Crowley would have had access to Bennett's private rituals, as Bennett left them with him on leaving England. (Bennett wrote an invocation with a similar purpose, "The Magical Invocation of the Higher Genius" (ibid., p. 198), that does not rely on Goodwin.) Israel Regardie gave a version derived from the *Goetia* in *The Tree of Life* (1932; rpt. New York: Weiser, 1972), pp. 266–268, and later composed an elaborated version, "The Bornless Ritual for the Invocation of the Higher Genius," first published in *The Golden Dawn* (1937–40; 6th rev. ed., St. Paul: Llewellyn, 1993), vol. III, p. 259. In 1921 Crowley prepared a revision of the *Goetia* version with an initiated gloss, "Liber Samekh sub figura 800," published in *Book Four, Part III*, Appendix IV.

[40] He does so in a note to his personal copy of the *Goetia*, given on p. 98 infra.

[41] Crowley noted that "demons are usually described as resembling animals or distortions of them," in his *The Scented Garden of Abdullah the Satirist of Shiraz (Bagh-i-muattar)* (privately printed, 1910); facs. rpt., with introduction by M.P. Starr (Chicago: Teitan, 1991), p. 38; the note gives a first-hand account of the 49 Abramelin servitors of Beelzebub.

[42] *The Chaldæan Oracles as Set Down by Julianus*, trans. Francesco Patrizzi and Thomas Stanley (Gillette, NJ: Heptangle, 1989), §301. Michael Psellus comments that "there are certain Names among all Nations delivered to them by God, which have an unspeakable power in Divine Rites," and cautions against translating these from language to language (p. 70).

A distinction was observed in classical Greece between "high" magic or *theurgia* (θεουργία), and "low" magic or *goetia*, and in later times this distinction was enforced. Apollonius of Tyana (1st century E.V.) stood trial for miracle-working by the aid of demons, and Philostratus, writing later in his defense, distinguished between the magic of a *goetes* (γόης) or wizard, and that of a *magus* (μάγος), i.e. a theurgist like the *magi* with whom Apollonius studied in Babylon. Apuleius (2nd century E.V.), who also stood trial for sorcery, considered *dæmones* to be visible gods, immortal intermediary ærial spirits confined to the sublunary atmosphere that govern magical operations and divination. Spiritual needs, like the invocation of one's genius or *daimon* could be legitimately addressed through theurgy, but the counsel of *The Chaldæan Oracles* (§241) is to "enlarge not thy destiny" and trust in fate and providence. Crowley's adjuration that the Guardian Angel be attained (*theurgia*) before lesser works of magic are worked (*goetia*) resolves this ancient dilemma.

Everyday needs gave rise to *goetia*, and although the present work went into circulation some 1,500 years after Apollonius and Apuleius, it is rooted in an old tradition. Its spirits offer a means of improving one's lot in life, addressing the entire spectrum of human concerns, from preferment and wealth to sex and knowledge.

☦ ☦ ☦

The historical Solomon was King David's son by Bathsheba, and ruled Israel in the tenth century B.C.E. He has long had a reputation as a wise and powerful magician capable of controlling demons. The first century B.C.E. pseudepigraphical *Testament of Solomon* tells of his building of the Temple of Solomon by magic and the use of demons. The first century E.V. historian Flavius Josephus writes of Solomon that:

> He was in no way inferior to the Egyptians, who are said to have been beyond all men in understanding; nay, indeed, it is evident that their sagacity was very much inferior to that of the king's. ... God also enabled him to learn that skill which expels demons, which is a science useful and sanitive to men. He composed such incantations also by which distempers are alleviated. And he left behind him the manner of using exorcisms, by which they drive away demons.[43]

Josephus described witnessing a contemporary, Eleazar, use the ring of Solomon to expel a demon in the presence of the emperor Vespasian and his Roman court.

A gnostic Nag Hammadi text describes the creation of 49 androgynous demons whose "names and functions you will find in 'The Book of Solomon'"—perhaps the earliest surviving reference to a Solomonic catalogue of demons.[44] The German author Kiesewetter suggests that *Lemegeton*—the name of the compilation of which the *Goetia* is a part—was the name of a magician belonging to a Gnostic sect, but there is no evidence that a magician of that name ever existed.[45]

---

[43] Flavius Josephus, *Antiquities of the Jews*, viii, 2, 5, trans. William Whiston (Cincinnati: Applegate, 1855), p. 216.

[44] "On the Origin of the World," in James M. Robinson, gen. ed., *The Nag Hammadi Library in English* (San Francisco: Harper & Row, 1977), p. 167.

[45] Karl Kiesewetter, *Faust in der Geschichte und Tradition. Mit besonderer Berücksichtigung des okkulten Phänomenalismus und des mittelalterlichen Zauberwesens* (Berlin: Hermann Barsdorf Verlag, 1921). With the confidence afforded by ignorance of classical Greek, I suggest the possible reading "very powerful sound" for *lemegeton*.

Solomonic magical works exist in Hebrew but are of uncertain date and provenance.[46] Solomon entered Arabic folklore in *The Arabian Nights*[47] as Sulemain, and
the demons became the *jinn* or genies who have the power to grant wishes when
released from the vessel in which they were sealed. Solomon and his seal are also
mentioned in the *Picatrix* (*Gayat al-Hakim*), an Arabic work on astrological and tal-
ismanic magic that was translated into Spanish and Latin in early mediæval Spain,[48]
where this magical tradition entered Europe. Michael Scot, who studied in Spain in
this period, described a book whose spirits clamored when the volume was opened:

> What do you want? What do you seek? What do you order? Say what you want
> and it shall be done forthwith.[49]

Solomonic magical books have been frowned upon since William of Auvergne,
bishop of Paris (d. 1249), and the genre has had little scholarly attention. The only
English academic to examine the *Goetia* in any depth adopted a prejudicial attitude
that would have done credit to a medieval prelate.[50] Other English authors who have
examined the *Goetia* are A.E. Waite and Sayed Idries Shah,[51] and more recently,
Robert Turner.[52] German scholars have produced serious scholarship on magical gri-
moires, but they tell us little of the *Goetia*, as the Solomonic compilation entitled
Lemegeton differs in German-speaking countries, where the place of *Goetia* or lesser
Key of Solomon as part one of the compilation is occupied by the greater *Key*.

---

[46] In a note to the text of Josephus quoted above, Whiston refers to early magical texts of
Solomon, citing J. A. Fabricius, *Codex Pseudepigraphus Veteris Testamenti* (Hamburg: Fel-
giner, 1722–33), p. 1054. Peter Friedrich Arpe also cites Josephus in connection with a sup-
posed 1st century C.E. Hebrew *Clavicula Salomonis* in *De prodigiosis naturæ et artis
operibus, talismanes et amuleta dictis* (Hamburg: Liebezeit, 1717). Johann Christian Wolf
believed he had examined this MS., citing it as מפתח שלמה (*Maphteah Shelomo*), of unknown
provenance or date, 48 quarto pp., in *Bibliotheca Hebræa*, vol. I (Hamburg, 1715–1733),
pp. 1047–1048. Hermann Gollancz published a study of a longer manuscript of later date
entitled מפתח שלמה, *Clavicula Salomonis* (Frankfurt: Kauffmann, and London: Nutt, 1903),
and issued a facsimile edition, ספר מפתח שלמה, *Sepher Maphteah Shelomo, Book of the Key
of Solomon* (London: Oxford University Press, 1914). Gedaliah ibn Jahya (partly paraphras-
ing Josephus) writes in the Hebrew *Shalsheleth-Hakabala* that Solomon was "the author of
writings and conjurations against Evil Agents in a work called *The Key of Solomon*," possibly the earliest reference to this particular title; quoted in Gollancz, op. cit., p. iii.

[47] *The Thousand and One Nights*, or *Alf laila wa-laila*; numerous editions exist.

[48] *Picatrix: The Latin Version of the Ghayat Al-Hakim*, edited by David Pingree (London:
Warburg Institute, 1986); the *Picatrix* is at this writing unavailable in English. It has a section
that bears a structural similarity to the *Goetia*, characterizing the magical influences of the
seven planets in the 36 zodiacal decans, each with associated descriptive images. The *Goetia*
characterizes the decans as personified spirits, and doubles the number to 72 by allowing a
spirit for day and night. The *Goetia* and *Picatrix* images are tabulated separately in Crowley,
Liber 777 (London, 1909; rev. ed, 1955), rpt. with additions as *777 and other Qabalistic
Writings* (York Beach, ME: Weiser, 1977, 1993); for the *Goetia* see cols. clvi, clviii, clx, clxii,
clxiv and clxvi; for the *Picatrix* see cols. cxlix, cl and cli.

[49] Lynn Thorndike, *Michael Scot* (London: Nelson, 1965), p. 120.

[50] E.M. Butler, *Ritual Magic* (Cambridge: Cambridge University Press, 1949, 1980).

[51] A.E. Waite, *Book of Black Magic and of Pacts*, cited in note 2 above; rev. ed. *The Book of
Ceremonial Magic* (1911; rpt. New Hyde Park, NY: University Books, 1992); see chap. 4.
See also Idries Shah, *The Secret Lore of Magic* (New York: Citadel Press, 1958), ch. 10.

[52] Robert Turner, *Elizabethan Magic* (Dorset: Element, 1989), pp. 139–141.

There are several English examples of the *Lemegeton* in the British Museum. All collate closely except that some have four parts, others five.[53] Each part has a different provenance. The *Goetia*'s spirits were first published by a reputed student of Cornelius Agrippa, Johann Weyer, in his *Pseudomonarchia Dæmonum* (1577).[54] This was quickly translated into English, with variants, in Reginald Scot's *Discoverie of Witchcraft* (1584).[55] Both versions differ in significant ways from the *Goetia* as published here. The second part, *Theurgia-Goetia*, agrees closely with the first part of the *Steganographia* of Trithemius (d. 1516).[56] The titles of the third, fourth and fifth parts, *Ars Paulina*, *Ars Almadel*, and *Ars Notaria* (more usually *Notoria*) are all attested in earlier manuscripts, some dating to the early mediæval period. Analysis of these texts must await scholarly editions of the *Lemegeton* and its component texts.[57] As Keith Thomas notes, "it would be a long ... task to trace the evolution of these different formulæ and establish the precise genealogy linking the many different essays in the 'notory art.'"[58] The "Preliminary Definition of Magic" (page 21) was adapted from Robert Turner's translation of Michael Maier.[59]

Crowley probably began work on the *Goetia* in 1901 as he remarks that it took three years to produce. It appeared in 1904 under the imprint of his Society for the Propagation of Religious Truth, Boleskine, Foyers, Inverness, Scotland.[60] An American piracy was issued in 1916 by the inimitable L. W. de Laurence, described by Crowley as a "Yankee thief."[61] Several facsimile editions have also appeared.[62]

---

[53] The present editor consulted Sloane MSS. 2731, 3825 and 3648, dating to the late 16th–early 17th c., the Baroque literary period; all are entitled *The Little Key of Solomon*—not "lesser." Mathers mentions a private codex; Crowley's reference to a variant reading from the "quartos" was an editorial jest. A thorough survey of MSS. has not been made for this edition.

[54] Published with *De Præstigiis Dæmonum* (Latin ed., Basilæ, 1577).

[55] First edition London: William Brome, 1584; facsimile reprint, Amsterdam: Theatrum Orbis Terrarum, and New York: Da Capo Press, 1971.

[56] Johannes Trithemius, *Steganographia* (Darmstadii, 1606); a partial English translation is *The Steganographia* (Edinburgh: Magnum Opus Hermetic Sourceworks, 1982).

[57] There are three editions of the *Lemegeton* in English, none of which examine its textual origins. The first is a facsimile with transcription of the five-part Sloane MS. 2731 entitled *Lemegeton; Clavicula Salomonis: or The Complete Lesser Key of Solomon the King*, ed. Nelson and Anna White (Pasadena, CA: privately printed, 1979). The second is based on the four-part Sloane MS. 3648: *The Lemegetton* [sic], *A Medieval Manual of Solomonic Magic*, ed. Kevin Wilby, Hermetic Research Series 5 (Lampeter, Wales, 1985). The third, also based on Sloane MS. 2731, is *Lemegeton: the Complete Lesser Key of Solomon*, ed. Wade Long (Hayward, CA: Seventh Ray Tools, 1996).

[58] Keith Thomas, *Religion and the Decline of Magic* (New York: Scribner's, 1971), p. 229.

[59] Michael Maier, *Laws of the Fraternity of the Rosie Crosse (Themis Aurea)* [trans. Robert Turner] (London, 1656; rpt. Los Angeles, CA: Philosophical Research, 1976), pp. 89–91.

[60] One copy was vellum (Crowley's own copy); ten were on Japanese vellum with a cream binding, and 200 copies on machine-made paper with black camel-hair paper wrappers.

[61] *The Lesser Key of Solomon. Goetia. The Book of Evil Spirits* (Chicago: de Laurence, Scott, 1916). De Laurence takes credit as editor and terms it the "only authorized edition extant."

[62] The first facsimile edition was issued by Jimmy Page (London: Equinox, 1976); although issued in hardcover, the dustjacket used camel-hair paper and it remains the facsimile most faithful to the 1904 original. A later facsimile was published by the late Herman Slater (New York: Magickal Childe, 1992). Anthony Naylor of the Mandrake Press issued a facsimile that combined Crowley's annotated and illustrated vellum copy and G.J. Yorke's copy that with transcripts of Crowley's notes (Thame, Oxon: Mandrake Press, 1993).

In 1924 E.V. Crowley conducted further magical operations with the spirit Belial, whom he referred to as "my own special ΔAIMON." His diary for 1924 preserves a ritual entitled "The Brazen Head"; his postscript note to p. 64 referring to an increase in Belial's subordinate spirits as a result of his work dates from this period.[63]

The present book is really a second edition of Crowley's, and editorial changes were kept to a minimum; these are detailed below.[64]

For research material and assistance I would like to thank the Warburg Institute at the University of London; the British Museum; the Harry Ransom Humanities Research Center, the University of Texas at Austin; Duke University Library Special Collections; the Bibliothèque Nationale de France; the Center for Research Libraries, Chicago; the Widener Library, Harvard; and the Mandrake Press.

Randall Bowyer gave invaluable editorial advice on Greek and Latin questions, and with J. Daniel Gunther gave valuable advice on the handling of the Preliminary Invocation; David Scriven and Clive Harper provided bibliographic advice; William E. Heidrick generously loaned his microfilms of the British Museum Sloane MSS.; Philippe Pissier, Matthieu Leon and Frederic MacParthy assisted with French grimoire sources; Eamonn Loughran provided valuable original research into London Papyrus 46 as well as the MS. copy used in this edition; Anthony Naylor of the Mandrake Press provided copies from Crowley's annotated *Goetia*; Marc Schneider proofread the revised Enochian; Marcus Jungkurth provided valuable research into German sources; Keith Schürholz suggested several fruitful lines of research; and Martin P. Starr gave sound advice and encouragement. I am also indebted to Randall Bowyer and Robin D. Matthews for their expert reading of the proofs.

This edition is dedicated to the memory of Frater Nia, Gerald Joseph Yorke.

— HYMENAEUS BETA
Frater Superior, O.T.O.

---

[63] This ritual appears in *The Magical Link* IX(3) (new series), Fall 1995 (Fairfax, CA: O.T.O.).

[64] For the sake of organization a few sections were given headings lacking in the first edition. Editorial notes in brackets give translations, citations, and occasional notes on the editorial handling of supplementary material. Crowley's later annotations to his personal copies of the *Goetia* have been added, demarcated following the editorial conventions on page xi.

The first edition gave Hebrew versions of the spirit-names from the Rudd manuscripts in the British Museum. *Liber 777* gave very different Hebrew versions. Both are given in tables as an appendix to this edition, with Rudd's Hebrew given in brackets. Other supplementary data is given from the *Goetia*, with astrological data from *Liber 777*.

The first edition grouped the figures on three pages; in this edition they have been renumbered and distributed in the text. A few were omitted as they pertained to the second part of the *Lemegeton* (*Theurgia-Goetia*). The engravings of several of the spirits by Louis Breton first appeared in Collin de Plancy's *Dictionnaire Infernal* (6th edition, 1863). Crowley's own drawings from his personal copy of the *Goetia* are also included.

The redaction of the Preliminary Invocation corrects errors introduced in the 1994 edition of Crowley's *Magick (Book 4, Parts I–IV)*, and is supplemented by a transcription of the Greek with Goodwin's English translation, as well as a facsimile of the portion of the original London Papyrus 46 containing the more difficult and frequently disputed readings.

The "Explanation of Certain Names" on p. 90 was augmented from Sloane MS. 2731.

The Enochian translations of the conjurations were very flawed in the first edition. This edition provides the Elizabethan Enochian in script and transliteration, with an "improved" G.D. transliteration; although considered obsolete by many, care was taken to provide an accurate G.D. pronunciation guide. Editorial procedures and sources

GOETIA

K	O	D	S	E	LI	M
O						
H						
A						
B						
I						O
M					O	K

ΕΠΙΚΑΛΟΥΜΑΙ ΣΕ ΤΟΝ ΕΝ ΤΩ ΚΕΝΕΩ ΠΝΕΥΜΑΤΙ, ΔΕΙΝΟΝ, ΑΟΡΑΤΟΝ, ΠΑΝΤΟΚΡΑΤΟΡΑ, ΘΕΟΝ ΘΕΩΝ, ΦΘΟΡΟΠΟΙΟΝ, ΚΑΙ ΕΡΗΜΟΠΟΙΟΝ, Ο ΜΙΣΩΝ ΟΙΚΙΑΝ ΕΥΣΤΑΘΟΥΣΑΝ, ΩΣ ΕΞΕΒΡΑΣΘΗΣ ΕΚ ΤΗΣ ΑΙΓΥΠΤΟΥ ΚΑΙ ΕΞΩ ΧΩΡΑΣ. ΕΠΟΝΟΜΑΣΘΗΣ Ο ΠΑΝΤΑ ΡΗΣΣΩΝ ΚΑΙ ΜΗ ΝΙΚΩΜΕΝΟΣ.

ΕΠΙΚΑΛΟΥΜΑΙ ΣΕ ΤΥΦΩΝ ΣΗΘ ΤΑΣ ΣΑΣ ΜΑΝΤΕΙΑΣ ΕΠΙΤΕΛΩ, ΟΤΙ ΕΠΙΚΑΛΟΥΜΑΙ ΣΕ ΤΟ ΣΟΝ ΑΥΘΕΝΤΙΚΟΝ ΣΟΥ ΟΝΟΜΑ ΕΝ ΟΙΣ ΟΥ ΔΥΝΗ ΠΑΡΑΚΟΥΣΑΙ ΙΩΕΡΒΗΘ, ΙΩΠΑΚΕΡΒΗΘ, ΙΩΒΟΛΧΩΣΗΘ, ΙΩΠΑΤΑΘΝΑΞ, ΙΩΣΩΡΩ, ΙΩΝΕΒΟΥΤΟΣΟΥΑΛΗΘ, ΑΚΤΙΩΦΙ, ΕΡΕΣΧΙΓΑΛ, ΝΕΒΟΠΟΩΑΛΗΘ, ΑΒΕΡΑΜΕΝΘΩΟΥ, ΛΕΡΘΕΞΑΝΑΞ, ΕΘΡΕΛΥΩΘ, ΝΕΜΑΡΕΒΑ, ΑΕΜΙΝΑ, ΟΛΟΝ ΗΚΕ ΜΟΙ ΚΑΙ ΒΑΔΙΣΟΝ ΚΑΙ ΚΑΤΑΒΑΛΕ ΤΟΝ ΔΕΙΝΟΝ ΜΑΘΕΡΣ. ΡΙΓΕΙ ΚΑΙ ΠΥΡΕΙΩ ΑΥΤΟΣ ΗΔΙΚΗΣΕΝ ΤΟΝ ΑΝΘΡΩΠΟΝ ΚΑΙ ΤΟ ΑΙΜΑ ΤΟΥ ΦΥΩΝΟΣ ΕΞΕΧΥΣΕΝ ΠΑΡ' ΕΑΥΤΩ.

ΔΙΑ ΤΟΥΤΟ ΤΑΥΤΑ ΠΟΙΕΩ ΚΟΙΝΑ.*

---

* I invoke Thee, the Terrible, Invisible, Almighty God of Gods, Who dwellest in the Void Place of the Spirit, Maker of Destruction, Maker of Desolation, O Thou Who hatest a calm household, for Thou wast cast out of Ægypt and out of Thy proper place.

Thou wast named He Who destroyeth all things and is not conquered.

I invoke Thee Typhon Seth: I carry out Thine oracular rites, for I invoke Thee by Thine own Potent Name of Thyself in words which Thou canst not misunderstand: Iôerbêth, Iôpakerbêth, Iôbolchôsêth, Iôpatathnax, Iôsôrô, Iôneboutosoualêth, Aktiôphi, Ereschigal, Nebopoôalêth, Aberamenthôou, Lerthexanax, Ethreluôth, Nemareba, Aëmina. Come wholly to me and go and strike down the terrible Mathers. With frost and fire he hath wronged Man, and the blood of Phuôn he hath poured out by his side.

Because of this I do these public deeds.

2

Prefatory Note

A.G.R.C.   A.R.C.G.

THIS translation of the First Book of the "Lemegeton" (now for the first time made accessible to English adepts and students of the Mysteries) was done, after careful collation and edition, from numerous MSS. in Hebrew, Latin, French and English, by G. H. Fra. D.D.C.F., by the order of the Secret Chief of the Rosicrucian Order.[1] The G. H. Fra., having succumbed unhappily to the assaults of the Four Great Princes (acting notably under Martial influences), it seemed expedient that the work should be brought to its conclusion by another hand. The investigations of a competent Skryer into the house of our unhappy Fra., confirmed this divination; neither our Fra. nor his Hermetic Mul. were there seen; but only the terrible shapes of the evil Adepts S.V.A.[2] and

---

[1] Mr. A. E. Waite writes (*Real History of the Rosicrucians*, p. 426): "I beg leave to warn my readers that all persons who proclaim themselves to be Rosicrucians are simply members of pseudo-fraternities, and that there is that difference between their assertion and the fact of the case in which the essence of a lie consists!"

It is within the Editor's personal knowledge that Mr. Waite was (and still is probably) a member of a society claiming to be the R.C. fraternity.

As Mr. Waite constantly hints in his writings that he is in touch with initiated centres, I think the syllogism, whose premisses are given above, is fair, if not quite formal.—ED.

[2] It was owing to our Fra. receiving this S.V.A. as his Superior, and giving up the Arcana of our Fraternity into so unhallowed a power, that We decided no longer to leave Our dignity and authority in the hands of one who could be thus easily imposed upon. (For by a childish and easy magical trick did S.V.A. persuade D.D.C.F. of that lie.)

H., whose original bodies having been sequestered by Justice, were no longer of use to them. On this we stayed no longer Our Hand; but withdrawing Ourselves, and consulting the Rota, and the Books M. and Q. did decide to ask Mr. Aleister Crowley,[1] a poet, and skilled student of Magical Lore, and an expert Kabbalist, to complete openly that which had been begun in secret.[2] This is that which is written: "His Bishoprick let another take." And again: "Oculi Tetragrammaton."[3] This is also that which is said: "Nomen Secundum קרע שטן refertur ad *Gebhurah*; qui est *Rex* secundus, quo moriente *delabebantur Posteriora Matris*, unde *Bittul* atque Corruptio *Achurajim Patris et Matris* hoc nomine[4] indigitatur."[5]

And so saying we wish you well.

> Ex Deo Nascimur.
> In Jesu Morimur.
> Per S.S. Reviviscimus.[6]

Given forth from our Mountain of A., this day of C.C. 1903 A.D.

---

[1] The task of editing the MSS. thus placed in my hands has proved practically a sinecure. The original translator and editor had completed his work so efficiently that very little was left for me to do beyond undertaking the business transactions connected with it, reading the proofs, and deciphering, with transliteration from the Enochian characters, the "Angelic" version of Perdurabo, from the priceless MS. entrusted to me.—ED.

[2] He that is appointed to complete in secret that which had been begun openly is R.R., and to be heard of at the care of the Editor.

[3] ["Eyes of the Lord."]

[4] [This word omitted in the first edition.]

[5] ["The second name [of the 42-fold name of God], קרע שטן, is referred to Geburah, who is the second King, at the time of whose dying the hindparts of the Mother were sinking down, whence Bittul [lit. "destruction"] and even the corruption of the Achurajim [lit. "hindparts"] of the Father and Mother are invoked by this name." Christian Knorr von Rosenroth, *Kabbala denudata* (2 vol.) (Sulzbachi: Typis Abrahami Lichtenthaleri, 1677–84), p. 505.]

[6] ["From God we are born, In Jesus we die, Through the Holy Spirit we come to life again." *Fama Fraternitatis*, 1614.]

Preliminary Invocation

The Invocation of the Heart
Girt with a Serpent,
or, The Bornless Ritual

Thee I invoke, the Bornless one.[1]
Thee, that didst create the Earth and the Heavens:[2]
Thee, that didst create the Night and the day.
Thee, that didst create the darkness and the Light.
Thou art Osorronophris:[3] Whom no man hath seen at any time.
Thou art Iäbas:[4]
Thou art Iäpōs:[5]
Thou hast distinguished between the just and the Unjust.
Thou didst make the female and (the) Male.[6]
Thou didst produce the Seed and the Fruit.[7]
Thou didst form Men to love one another, and to hate one another.[8]

---

1. (ΑΠΕ ΠΥΡ. The Bornless Fire = 666.)
2. (*K'un* [☷] and *Ch'ien* [☰].)
3. (Asar-Un-Nefer.) <Osorronophris = the perfected Osiris. The hierophant in the G.D. neophyte ritual. But for those who accept Θελημα variation, the formula is of Horus, conquering child, not dying god. Candidate ∴ is Horus, & the perfected Horus is Ra Hoor Khuit.>
4. <Ia-Besz. Life, Bread, Flesh.>
5. <Ia-Apophrasz. Love, Wine, Blood.>
6. <Involution.>
7. <Evolution.>
8. <Self realization.>

I am _____[9] Thy Prophet, unto Whom Thou didst commit Thy Mysteries, the Ceremonies of _____:[9]

Thou didst produce the moist and the dry, and that[10] which nourisheth all created Life.

Hear Thou Me, for I am the Angel of (Apophrasz)[11] Osorronophris: this is Thy True Name, handed down to the Prophets of _____.[9]

א

< △ E. *Golden Glory.*

Tahaoeloj 𝕋

☆ יהוה

Shu supporting sky 2°=9° >

Hear Me:—

Ar: Thiao:[12] ⊦Reibet⊣:[13] Atheleberseth:[14]
A: Blatha:[15] Abeu: ⊦Eben⊣: Phi:[16]
⊦Chitasoe⊣:[17] Ib:[18] Thiao.

---

9. [Goodwin gives Μούσης and Ἰστραηλ, transliterated in the first edition as Mosheh and Ishrael. Crowley changed these to "Ankh-f-n-Khonsu" and "Khem" (i.e. Egypt) and instructed that each magician should personalize the ritual with his or her own names; see "Liber Samekh," *Magick (Book 4, Parts I-IV)*, p. 513. They are left blank in the text for this reason.]

10. (Eagle, Lion & Elixir.)

11. [In his vellum *Goetia* Crowley crossed out "Paphro" (the original Greek had Φαπρο, *phapro*), and inserted "Apophrasz"; the text given here has been changed accordingly. Crowley gave an alternate reading for "Paphro Osorronophris" as "Apophi-Asar-un-nefer," which parallels Crowley's note to "Osorronophris" given above. The Yorke *Goetia* has the reading Crowley later used in "Liber Samekh," "Ptah-Apophrasz-Ra," either taken from the second annotated *Goetia* or interpolated from "Liber Samekh" by Yorke.]

12. <טיאו = 26.>

13. (Ῥαβδος [wand]. Ρη Βητ = 418. The Flux Mercury. *Spiritus verbi.*)

14. (את-אל-באר-שט. The Essence of AL the scion of SET (Hadit). 401+31+203+31 ((☉))=666.)

15. (BLAThA ב. Balata = Justice (Enochian [V⸮CↃ])=♎ Card[inal] Sign of △.)

16. (*Phi* = Φι = 510 = Binah (Νυξ, Θυρα, Κρονος &c).)

17. (Ἥλιος [=] 318 [= Θητα]. Θητα-Cυ. Soul (begetter) of ☉.) [Crowley's qabalistic analysis was based on the variant and possibly corrupted reading "Thitasoe" in the first edition.]

18. (IB = ♍ ☿ Virgin of Hermes. The unsullied Vehicle of the Word.)

[*Rubric*]

Hear Me, and make all Spirits subject unto Me: so that every Spirit of the Firmament and of the Ether: upon the Earth and under the Earth: on dry Land and in the Water: of Whirling Air, and of rushing Fire: and every Spell and Scourge of God may be obedient unto Me.[19]

שׁ

< △ S. *Red are the Rays.*

Ohooohaatan ☀

✡ אלהים

Thoum æsh neith 4°=7□ >

I invoke Thee, the Terrible and Invisible God: Who dwellest in the Void Place of the Spirit:—

Arogogorobraō: ⌐Sochou⌐:[20]
Modoriō: ⌐Phalarchaō⌐: Oöö:[21] Apé,[22] The Bornless One:
Hear Me: etc.

---

19. < *Firmament:*   1. The רוח. Mental Plane. Zeus. Shu. Where revolves the wheel of the *gunas.* s[attva]. r[ajas]. t[amas]. ☿ ♁ ♃.

    Ether: 2. *Ākāśa.* Æthyr of physics. Receives, records, & transmits all impulses without suffering mutation thereby.

    Upon the Earth: 3. Sphere where 1 & 2 appear to perception (perceived projections).

    Under the Earth: 4. The world of those phenomena which inform 3.

    Dry Land: 5. Sphere of dead material things; (Dry = unknowable) ∴ unable to act on our minds.

    Water: 6. Vehicle whereby we feel such things (5).

    Whirling Air: 7. Menstruum wherein these feelings (6) are mentally apprehended, whirling instability of thought.

    Rushing Fire: 8. World in which 7 (wandering thought) burns up to swift darting will.

    9. Spell: any form of consciousness (idea).

    10. Scourge: any form of action (act).>

20. (HE is ☉. Coθ the South 279=9×31. Cf. σωτηρ.)

21. ("Nothing under its three forms".) ["Liber Trigrammaton sub figura XXVII"].

22. (ʿΑΠΗ=ʿα-πη, not-where, i.e. the Bornless One. "I that go" "nowhere found" AIN SOPH.)

מ

< ▽ W. *Blue Radiance.*

Thahebyobeeatan ✠

☆ אל

Auramoth 3°=8° >

Hear Me:—

Roubriaō: Mariōdam: Balbnabaoth:[23] Assalonai: Aphniaō:
I: ˩Thōleth˥:[24] Abrasax: Aëōōü: Ischure, Mighty and Bornless
One!
Hear Me: etc.

ת

< ▽ N. *Green Flame.*

Thahaaotahe ✝

☆ אדני

Set fighting 1°=10° >

I invoke Thee:—

Ma: Barraiō:[25] Iōēl:[26] Kotha:[27]
Athorēbalō: Abraoth:
Hear Me: etc.

---

23. (בל בן אב אות Lord of the Son of the Sire of the Sign.)
24. (Thoteth = Fem[inine] of Thoth ▽ twin of △ as transmitter.) [Crowley's analysis
    was based on the corrupt reading "Thoteth," given here as "Tholeth."]
25. (Bar-Ra-Io   Son of the Sun, all Hail! ? βαρυ.)
26. (Io-AL   Hail, AL !)
27. (Cup.)

אמן

<�֍

⊛

☆ אהיה

+. O[siris] Slain. L. I[sis] Mourning. V. T[yphon].
x. O[siris] R[isen] >

Hear me![28]

Aōth:[29] Abaōth:[30] Basum:[31] Isak:[32]
Sabaoth:[33] Iao:

This is the Lord of the Gods:
This is the Lord of the Universe:
This is He Whom the Winds fear.

This is He, Who having made Voice by His Commandment, is Lord
of All Things; King, Ruler and Helper.

Hear Me: etc.

Hear Me:—[34]

Ieou: Pūr: Iou: Pūr:[35] Iaōt: Iaeō: Ioou: Abrasax: Sabriam:
Oo: Uu: ⟦Eu: Oo: Uu:⟧ ⟨Adōnai:⟩ Ede: Edu: ⊦Angelos tou
theou⊣: ⟨Analala⟩ Lai:[36] Gaia: ⊦Apa: Diachanna: Chorun.⊣[37]

---

28. ⟨Erect [drawing of Pyramid]. "Thou who art I &c."⟩ [These are probably
working notes from a rite in which Crowley interwove several texts. The pyra-
mid (which recurs below) suggests the opening of "Liber 671," and can also
signify the phallus; these readings are not mutually exclusive. The quotation is
from the Anthem of "Liber 800, The Ship," which is also referenced later.]
29. ⟨The Sign אות =407=11 × 37.⟩
30. ⟨ABA-oth. ABA = 4 also 1–2–1, O–I–O, ♀ Father, 82× 5.⟩
31. ⟨BA-SUM אב Father-Goer סום 666 Sol.⟩
32. ⟨ISAK יסאך 91= אמן &c. ישאך [thine] essence.⟩
33. ⟨Sabaoth = the 7= צבא (93) [+]ות (406) [=] 499 Aoth 407 = 37×11 signum.⟩
34. ⟨Rise in [drawing of Pyramid]. [For] of the Father & the Son &c.⟩ [See note 28.]
35. ⟨ΠϜρ=Fire=186=2×93=6×31.⟩
36. ⟨The Battle-cry of the Host.⟩
37. ⟨The Shooting-forth (like Stars) of the Semen. Overflows.⟩

(1)   I am He! the Bornless Spirit! having sight in the Feet: Strong, and the Immortal Fire!

(2)   I am He! the Truth!

(3)   I am He! Who hate that evil should be wrought in the World!

(♌ ♍ 4 5)   I am He, that lighteneth and thundereth.

(6)   I am He, from whom is the Shower of the Life of Earth:

(♌ ♍ 7 8)   I am He, whose mouth ever flameth:

(9)   I am He, the Begetter and Manifester unto the Light:

(10)   I am He; the Grace of the World:

"The Heart Girt with a Serpent" is My Name! [38]

Come Thou forth, and follow Me: and make all Spirits subject unto Me so that every Spirit of the Firmament, and of the Ether: upon the Earth and under the Earth: on dry land, or in the Water: of whirling Air or of rushing Fire: and every Spell and Scourge of God, may be obedient unto me!

Iao:[39] Sabao:[40]

Such are the Words!

---

38. (Elixir.)

39. (He is IA =Eleven, the seed ⋅ of *aleph*, אלף =111, Bacchus diphues, Ζευς Αρρηνοθηλυς, Heru-pa-kraat. [א]= 831 Φαλλός, Πυραμις, ⸰𝍏✝ = Kether, Chokmah, Binah. [א] = Atu O. [א] = One.)

40. (He is 6: He is צבא = [93 = Θελημα =] will or He is *Saba'a* i.e. seven (Arabic).)

LONDON PAPYRUS 46 — GREEK TRANSCRIPTION[1]

Στήλη τοῦ Θεοῦ τοῦ ζωγρ. εἰς τὴν ἐπιστολήν.

Σὲ καλῶ, τὸν ἀκέφαλον, τὸν κτίσαντα γῆν καὶ οὐρανὸν, τὸν κτίσαντα νύκτα καὶ ἡμέραν, σὲ τὸν κτίσαντα φῶς καὶ σκότος. Σὺ εἶ Ὀσορόννωφρις, ὃν οὐδεὶς εἶδε πώποτε, σὺ εἶ Ἴαβας, σὺ εἶ Ἰάπως, σὺ διέκρεινας τὸ δίκαιον καὶ τὸ ἄδικον, σὺ ἐποίησας θῆλυ καὶ ἄρρεν, σὺ ἔδειξας σπορὰν καὶ καρποὺς, σὺ ἐποίησας τοὺς ἀνθρώπους ἀλληλοφιλεῖν καὶ ἀλληλομισεῖν. Ἐγώ εἰμι Μούσης ὁ προφήτης σου, ᾧ παρέδωκας τὰ μυστήριά σου τὰ συντελούμενα Ἰστράηλ, σὺ ἔδειξας ὑγρὸν καὶ ξηρὸν καὶ πᾶσαν τροφήν. Ἐπάκουσόν[2] μου· ἐγώ εἰμι ἄγγελος τοῦ Φάπρω Ὀσορόννωφρις, τοῦτό ἐστίν σου τὸ ὄνομα τὸ ἀλήθινον, τὸ παραδιδόμενον τοῖς προφήταις Ἰστράηλ. Ἐπάκουσόν μου, αρ . . . θιαω, ρειβετ, αθελεβερσηθ, α . . βλαθα, αβευ, εβεν, φι, χιτασοη, ιβ . . θιαω, εἰσάκουσόν μου καὶ ἀπόστρεψον τὸ δαιμόνιον τοῦτο. Ἐπικαλοῦμαί σε τὸν ἐν τῷ κενῷ πνεύματι δεινὸν καὶ ἀόρατον θεὸν, αρογογοροβραω, σοχου, μοδοριω, φαλαρχαω, οοο, απε, ἀκέφαλε, ἀπάλλαξον τὸν δεῖνα ἀπὸ τοῦ συνέχοντος αὐτὸν δαίμονος. Ρουβριαω, μαριωδαμ, βαλβναβαωθ, ασσαλωναι, αφνιαω, ι, θωληθ, αβρασαξ, αηοων, ἰσχυρὲ, ἀκέφαλε, ἀπάλλαξον τὸν δεῖνα ἀπὸ τοῦ συνέχοντος αὐτὸν δαίμονος. Μα, βαρραιω, ιωηλ, κοθα, αθορηβαλω, αβραωθ, ἀπάλλαξον τὸν δεῖνα. Αωθ, αβαωθ, βασυμ, ισακ, σαβαωθ, ιαω, οὗτός ἐστιν ὁ κύριος τῶν θεῶν, οὗτός ἐστιν ὁ κύριος τῆς οἰκουμένης, οὗτός ἐστιν ὃν οἱ ἄνεμοι φοβοῦνται, οὗτός ἐστιν ὁ ποιήσας φωνὴν προστάγματι ἑαυτοῦ, πάντων[3] κύριε, βασιλεῦ, δύναστα, βοηθὲ, σῶσον ψυχὴν, ιεου, πυρ, ιου, πυρ, ιαωτ, ιαηω, ιοου, αβρασαξ, σαβριαμ, οο, υυ, ευ, οο, υυ, αδωναιε, ηδε, εδυ, ἄγγελος τοῦ θεοῦ, ανλαλα, λαι, γαια, απα, διαχαννα, χορυν, ἐγώ εἰμι ὁ ἀκέφαλος δαίμων ἐν τοῖς ποσὶν ἔχων τὴν ὅρασιν, ἰσχυρὸς, τὸ πῦρ τὸ ἀθάνατον, ἐγώ εἰμι ἡ ἀλήθεια, ὁ μεισῶν ἀδικήματα γείνεσθαι ἐν τῷ κόσμῳ, ἐγώ εἰμι ὁ ἀστράπτων καὶ βροντῶν, ἐγώ εἰμι οὗ ἐστιν ὁ ἴδρως ὄμβρος ἐπιπείπτων ἐπὶ τὴν γῆν ἵνα ὀχεύη, ἐγώ εἰμι οὗ τὸ στόμα καίεται δι᾽ ὅλου, ἐγώ εἰμι ὁ γεννῶν καὶ ἀπογεννῶν, ἐγώ εἰμι ἡ χάρις τοῦ αἰῶνος, ὄνομά μοι καρδία περιεζωσμένη ὄφιν. Ἔξελθε καὶ ἀκολούθησον. Τελετὴ τῆς προκειμένης ποιήσεως. Γράψας τὰ ὀνόματα εἰς καινὸν χαρτάριον καὶ διατείνας ἀπὸ κροτάφου εἰς κρόταφον σεαυτοῦ, ἐντύγχανε πρὸς βορέαν τοῖς ϛ ὀνόμασι, λέγων· Ὑπόταξόν μοι πάντα τὰ δαιμόνια, ἵνα μοι ᾖ[4] ὑπήκοος πᾶς δαίμων οὐράνιος καὶ αἰθέριος καὶ ἐπίγειος καὶ ὑπόγειος καὶ χερσαῖος καὶ ἔνυδρος καὶ πᾶσα ἐπιπομπὴ καὶ μάστιξ[5] θεοῦ. Καὶ ἔσται σοι τὰ δαιμόνια πάντα ὑπήκοα. Ἐστὶν δὲ τὸ ἀγαθὸν ζῴδιον.

---

1. [This Greek transcription and the accompanying footnotes are from Charles Wycliffe Goodwin, *Fragment of a Græco-Egyptian Work upon Magic from a Papyrus in the British Museum* (Cambridge: Deighton; Macmillan; London: J.W. Parker; Oxford: J.H. Parker, 1852), pp. 6, 8.]
2. MS. επακουων.
3. MS. παντα.
4. MS. ην.
5. MS. μαστιξι.

LONDON PAPYRUS 46 — ENGLISH TRANSLATION[6]

An address to the god drawn upon the letter.

I call thee, the headless one, that didst create earth and heaven, that didst create night and day, thee the creator of light and darkness. Thou art Osoronnophris, whom no man hath seen at any time; thou art Iabas, thou art Iapōs, thou hast distinguished the just and the unjust, thou didst make female and male, thou didst produce seeds and fruits, thou didst make men to love one another and to hate one another. I am Moses thy prophet, to whom thou didst commit thy mysteries, the ceremonies of Israel; thou didst produce the moist and the dry and all manner of food. Listen to me: I am an angel of Phapro Osoronnophris; this is thy true name, handed down to the prophets of Israel. Listen to me, ... hear me and drive away this spirit.

I call thee the terrible and invisible god residing in the empty wind, ... thou headless one, deliver such an one from the spirit that possesses him. . . . . strong one, headless one, deliver such an one from the spirit that possesses him. . . . . deliver such an one . . . . This is the lord of the gods, this is the lord of the world, this is he whom the winds fear, this is he who made voice by his commandment, lord of all things, king, ruler, helper, save this soul . . . . angel of God . . . . I am the headless spirit, having sight in my feet, strong, the immortal fire; I am the truth; I am he that hateth that ill-deeds should be done in the world; I am he that lighteneth and thundereth; I am he whose sweat is the shower that falleth upon the earth that it may teem; I am he whose mouth ever burneth; I am the begetter and bringer forth (?); I am the Grace of the World; my name is the heart girt with a serpent. Come forth and follow. — The celebration of the preceding ceremony. — Write the names upon a piece of new paper, and having extended it over your forehead from one temple to the other, address yourself turning towards the north to the six names, saying: — Make all the spirits subject to me, so that every spirit of heaven and of the air, upon the earth and under the earth, on dry land and in the water, and every spell and scourge of God, may be obedient to me. — And all the spirits shall be obedient to you. . . . .

---

6.   [This translation is from Goodwin, op. cit., pp. 7, 9. The portion of the papyrus giving the barbarous names is provided as Figure 4 on p. 13.]

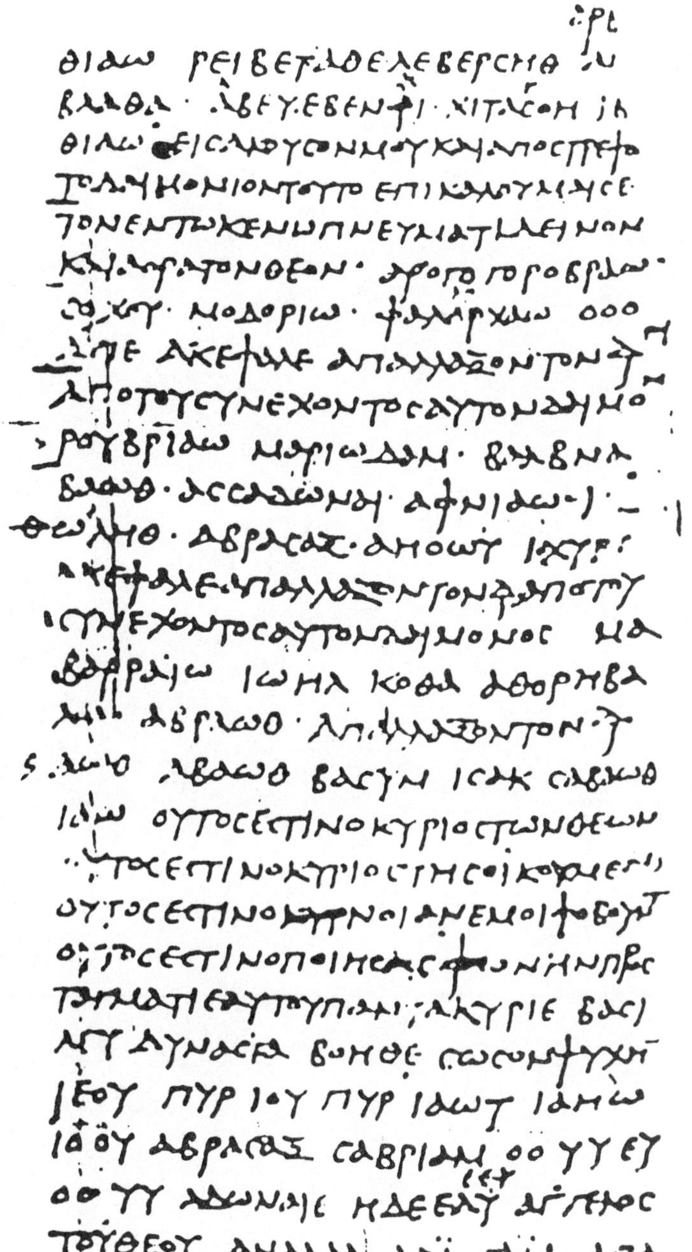

Figure 4. Excerpt from the London Magical Papyrus 46 showing the barbarous names of evocation. By courtesy of the British Museum.

The Initiated Interpretation
of Ceremonial Magic

INTRODUCTORY ESSAY BY ALEISTER CROWLEY

IT IS loftily amusing to the student of magical literature who is not quite a fool — and rare is such a combination! — to note the criticism directed by the Philistine against the citadel of his science. Truly, since our childhood has ingrained into us not only literal belief in the Bible, but also substantial belief in *Alf Laylah wa Laylah*,[1] and only adolescence can cure us, we are only too liable, in the rush and energy of dawning manhood, to overturn roughly and rashly both these classics, to regard them both on the same level, as interesting documents from the standpoint of folk-lore and anthropology, and as nothing more.

Even when we learn that the Bible, by a profound and minute study of the text, may be forced to yield up Qabalistic arcana of cosmic scope and importance, we are too often slow to apply a similar restorative to the companion volume, even if we are the lucky holders of Burton's veritable edition.

To me, then, it remains to raise the *Alf Laylah wa Laylah* into its proper place once more.

I am not concerned to deny the objective reality of all "magical" phenomena; if they are illusions, they are at least as real as many unquestioned facts of daily life; and, if we follow Herbert Spencer, they are at least evidence of *some* cause.[2]

---

[1] [*A Thousand and One Nights*, commonly called *The Arabian Nights*.]
[2] This, incidentally, is perhaps the greatest argument we possess, pushed to its extreme, against the Advaitist theories.

15

Now, this fact is our base. What is the cause of my illusion of seeing a spirit in the triangle of Art?

Every smatterer, every expert in psychology, will answer: "That cause lies in your brain."

English children are taught (*pace* the Education Act) that the Universe lies in infinite Space; Hindu children, in the *ākāśa*, which is the same thing.

Those Europeans who go a little deeper learn from Fichte, that the phenomenal Universe is the creation of the Ego; Hindus, or Europeans studying under Hindu *gurus*, are told, that by *ākāśa* is meant the *cit-ākāśa*. The *citākāśa* is situated in the "Third Eye," i.e., in the brain. By assuming higher dimensions of space, we can assimilate this fact to Realism; but we have no need to take so much trouble.

This being true for the ordinary Universe, that all sense-impressions are dependent on changes in the brain,[1] we must include illusions, which are after all sense-impressions as much as "realities" are, in the class of "phenomena dependent on brain-changes."

Magical phenomena, however, come under a special sub-class, since they are willed, and their cause is the series of "real" phenomena called the operations of ceremonial Magic.

These consist of

(1) Sight.

    The circle, square, triangle, vessels, lamps, robes, implements, etc.

(2) Sound.

    The invocations.

(3) Smell.

    The perfumes.

(4) Taste.

    The Sacraments.

(5) Touch.

    As under (1).

(6) Mind.

    The combination of all these and reflection on their significance.

---

[1] Thought is a secretion of the brain (Weissmann). Consciousness is a function of the brain (Huxley).—A.C.

These unusual impressions (1–5) produce unusual brain-changes; hence their summary (6) is of unusual kind. Its projection back into the apparently phenomenal world is therefore unusual.

Herein then consists the reality of the operations and effects of ceremonial magic,[1] and I conceive that the apology is ample, so far as the "effects" refer only to those phenomena which appear to the magician himself, the appearance of the spirit, his conversation, possible shocks from imprudence, and so on, even to ecstasy on the one hand, and death or madness on the other.

But can any of the effects described in this our book *Goetia* be obtained, and if so, can you give a rational explanation of the circumstances? Say you so?

I can, and will.

The spirits of the *Goetia* are portions of the human brain.

Their seals therefore represent (Mr. Spencer's projected cube) methods of stimulating or regulating those particular spots (through the eye).

The names of God are vibrations calculated to establish:

(a) General control of the brain. (Establishment of functions relative to the subtle world.)

(b) Control over the brain in detail. (Rank or type of the Spirit.)

(c) Control of one special portion. (Name of the Spirit.)[2]

The perfumes aid this through smell. Usually the perfume will only tend to control a large area; but there is an attribution of perfumes to letters of the alphabet enabling one, by a Qabalistic formula, to spell out the Spirit's name.

I need not enter into more particular discussion of these points; the intelligent reader can easily fill in what is lacking.

If, then, I say, with Solomon:

"The Spirit Cimieries[3] teaches logic," what I mean is:

"Those portions of my brain which subserve the logical faculty may be stimulated and developed by following out the processes called 'The Invocation of Cimieries.'"[4]

---

[1] Apart from its value in obtaining one-pointedness. On this subject the curious may consult my בראשית [*Berashith*].

[2] [The MS. of this essay, at the Harry Ransom Humanities Research Center, University of Texas at Austin, adds here: "through the ear."]

[3] [Cimeies, the sixty-sixth spirit of the *Goetia*.]

[4] [The MS. has this passage in an unknown language following here: "—*ham kitna khabai-ka-kajay-log is-batka tamasha karta ham lekh-mangta*."]

And this is a purely materialistic rational statement; it is independent of any objective hierarchy at all. Philosophy has nothing to say; and Science can only suspend judgment, pending a proper and methodical investigation of the facts alleged.

Unfortunately, we cannot stop there. Solomon promises us that we can (1) obtain information; (2) destroy our enemies; (3) understand the voices of nature; (4) obtain treasure; (5) heal diseases, etc. I have taken these five powers at random; considerations of space forbid me to explain all.

(1) Brings up facts from sub-consciousness.

(2) Here we come to an interesting fact. It is curious to note the contrast between the noble means and the apparently vile ends of magical rituals. The latter are disguises for sublime truths. "To destroy our enemies" is to realize the illusion of duality, to excite compassion.

(Ah! Mr. Waite,[1] the world of Magic is a mirror, wherein who sees muck is muck.)

(3) A careful naturalist will understand much from the voices of the animals he has studied long. Even a child knows the difference of a cat's miauling and purring. The faculty may be greatly developed.

(4) Business capacity may be stimulated.

(5) Abnormal states of the body may be corrected, and the involved tissues brought back to tone, in obedience to currents started from the brain.

So for all other phenomena. There is no effect which is truly and necessarily miraculous.

Our Ceremonial Magic fines down, then, to a series of minute, though of course empirical, physiological experiments, and whoso will carry them through intelligently need not fear the result.

I have all the health, and treasure, and logic I need; I have no time to waste. "There is a lion in the way."[2] For me these practices are useless; but for the benefit of others less fortunate I give them to the world, together with this explanation of, and apology for, them.

I trust that the explanation will enable many students who have hitherto, by a puerile objectivity in their view of the question, obtained no results, to succeed; that the apology may impress upon our scornful men of science that the study of the bacillus should give place to that

---

[1] < A poet of great ability. He edited a book called *Of Black Magic and of Pacts*, in which he vilifies the same. >

[2] [*Proverbs* 26:13.]

of the baculum,[1] the little to the great—how great one only realizes when one identifies the wand with the *mahāliṅga*,[2] up which Brahmā flew at the rate of 84,000 *yojanas* a second for 84,000 *mahākalpas*, down which Viṣṇu flew at the rate of 84,000 *crores* of *yojanas* a second for 84,000 *crores* of *mahākalpas*—yet neither reached an end.

But I reach an end.

BOLESKINE HOUSE
Foyers, N.B., July, 1903.

---

[1] [The MS. has "wand."]

[2] < The Phallus of Śiva the Destroyer. It is really identical with the Qabalistic "Middle Pillar" of the "Tree of Life." >

NOTE

I had intended in this place to devote a little attention to the edition (save the mark) of the *Goetia* produced by Mr. A.E. Waite in *The Book of Black Magic*.

But a fresh perusal of that work reveals it to be such a farrago of twenty-fifth-rate shoddy schoolboy journalism that disgust compels me to refrain. I may merely mention that the letterpress is garbled and the seals abominably drawn. To give one concrete example; on p. 202 Mr. Waite observes:

"This" (that the compiler of the *Lemegeton* was acquainted with the N.T.) "is proved by the references in the Third Conjuration to the Living Creatures of the Apocalypse."

There is no such reference!

In the Second Conjuration, for I have corrected Mr. Waite's careless blunder, there is a reference to Living Creatures; there is also a reference to the same beings in the Apocalypse.

The argument then stands:

The Book of Chronicles refers to King Solomon (unknown date).

Mr. Waite refers to King Solomon (1898),

Therefore,

The author of the Book of Chronicles was acquainted with Mr. Waite's book.[1]

We will conclude by condoling with the author of the Book of Chronicles.

---

[1] Even apart from this, if Living Creatures are really existent things—which the name would suggest—the argument stands:

    The Rig-Veda,

    The Old Testament,

    The Insidecompletuar Britanniaware,

    The Sword of Song

all refer to the Sun.

    ∴ there is a common source in literature.

    Mr. Waite's fallacy is all very well, though, for people who have never kept Living Creatures, nor even made a fourth at Bridge.

The Preliminary Definition of Magic[1]

MAGIC is the Highest, most Absolute, and most Divine Knowledge of Natural Philosophy, advanced in its works and wonderful operations by a right understanding of the inward and occult virtue of things; so that true Agents[2] being applied to proper Patients,[3] strange and admirable effects will thereby be produced. Whence magicians are profound and diligent searchers into Nature: they, because of their skill, know how to anticipate an effort,[4] the which to the vulgar shall seem to be a miracle.

Origen saith that the Magical Art doth not contain anything subsisting, but although it should, yet that it must not be Evil, or subject to contempt or scorn: and doth distinguish the *Natural Magic* from that which is *Diabolical*.

Apollonius Tyanæus only exercised the *Natural Magic*, by the which he did perform wonderful things.

Philo Hebræus saith that true Magic, by which we do arrive at the understanding of the Secret Works of Nature, is so far from being contemptible that the greatest Monarchs and Kings have studied it. Nay!

---

[1] This Preliminary Definition of Magic is found in very few Codices, and is probably later than the body of the work.

[2] Or Actives.

[3] Or Passives.

[4] Or Effect.

among the Persians none might reign unless he was skilful in this
GREAT ART.

This Noble Science often degenerateth, from *Natural* becometh
Diabolical, and from *True Philosophy* turneth unto *Nigromancy*.[1] The
which is wholly to be charged upon its followers, who, abusing or not
being capable of that High and Mystical Knowledge do immediately
hearken unto the temptations of *Sathan*, and are misled by him into the
Study of the *Black Art*. Hence it is that Magic lieth under disgrace, and
they who seek after it are vulgarly esteemed *Sorcerers*.

The Fraternity of the Rosie Crusians thought it not fit to style themselves Magicians, but rather Philosophers. And they be not ignorant
Empiricks,[2] but learned and experienced Physicians, whose remedies
be not only *Lawful* but *Divine*.

---

[1] Or the Black Art, as distinct from mere Necromancy, or Divination by the Dead.
[2] Or Quacks and Pretenders. Vide note on page 26.

The Brief Introductory Description

(N.B. This is taken from several MS. Codices, of which the four principal variations are here composed together in parallel columns as an example of the close agreement of the various texts of the *Lemegeton*.

For in the whole work the differences in the wording of the various Codices are not sufficient to require the constant giving of parallel readings; but except in the more ancient examples there is much deterioration in the Seals and Sigils, so that in this latter respect the more recent exemplars are not entirely reliable.)

CLAVICULA SALOMONIS REGIS,	THE WHOLE LEMEGETON OR CLAVICULA.	CLAVICULA SALOMONIS REGIS,	THE KEY OF SOLOMON.
which containeth all the Names, Offices, and Orders of all the Spirits that ever he had converse with, with the Seals and Characters to each Spirit and the manner of calling them forth to visible appearance: In 5 parts, viz.:	Now this Book containeth all the Names, Orders, and Offices of all the Spirits with which Solomon ever conversed, the Seals and Characters belonging to each Spirit, and the manner of calling them forth to visible appearance: Divided into 5 special Books or parts, viz.:	which containeth all the Names, Offices, and Orders of all the Spirits with whom he ever held any converse; together with the Seals and Characters proper unto each Spirit, and the method of calling them forth to visible appearance: In 5 parts, viz.:	which contains all the names, orders, and offices of all the Spirits that ever Solomon conversed with, together with the Seals and Characters belonging to each Spirit, and the manner of calling them forth to visible appearance: In 4 parts.

(1) THE FIRST PART is a Book of Evil Spirits, called GOËTIA, showing how he bound up those Spirits, and used them in general things, whereby he obtained great fame.

(2) THE SECOND PART is a Book of Spirits, partly Evil and partly Good, which is named THEURGIA-GOËTIA, all Aërial Spirits, etc.

(3) THE THIRD PART is of Spirits governing the Planetary Hours, and what Spirits belong to every degree, of the Signs, and Planets in the Signs. Called the PAULINE ART, etc.

(4) THE FOURTH PART of this Book is called ALMADEL OF SOLOMON, which containeth those Spirits which govern the Four Altitudes, or the 360 Degrees of the Zodiac.

These two last Orders of Spirits

(1) THE FIRST BOOK, or PART, which is a Book concerning Spirits of Evil, and which is termed THE GOËTIA OF SOLOMON, sheweth forth his manner of binding these Spirits for use in things divers. And hereby did he acquire great renown.

(2) THE SECOND BOOK is one which treateth of Spirits mingled of Good and Evil Natures, the which is entitled THE THEURGIA-GOËTIA, or the Magical Wisdom of the Spirits Aërial, whereof some do abide, but certain do wander and bide not.

(3) THE THIRD BOOK, called ARS PAULINA, or THE ART PAULINE, treateth of the Spirits allotted unto every degree of the 360 Degrees of the Zodiac; and also of the Signs, and of the Planets in the Signs, as well as of the Hours.

(4) THE FOURTH BOOK, called ARS ALMADEL SALOMONIS, or THE ART ALMADEL OF SOLOMON, concerneth those Spirits which be set over the Quaternary of the Altitudes.

These two last mentioned Books,

(1) THE FIRST PART is a Book of Evil Spirits, called GOËTIA, showing how he bound up those Spirits and used them in things general and several, whereby he obtained great fame.

(2) THE SECOND PART is a Book of Spirits partly Evil, and partly Good, which is called THEURGIA-GOËTIA, all Aërial Spirits, etc.

(3) THE THIRD PART is of Spirits governing the Planetary Hours, and of what Spirits do belong to every Degree of the Signs, and of the Planets in the Signs. This is called the PAULINE ART, etc.

(4) THE FOURTH PART of this Book is called ALMADEL OF SOLOMON, the which containeth those Spirits which do govern the Four Altitudes, or the 360 Degrees of the Zodiac.

These two last Orders of Spirits

(1) THE FIRST PART is a Book of Evil Spirits called GOËTIA, showing how he bound up those Spirits and used them in several things, whereby he obtained great fame.

(2) THE SECOND PART is a Book of Spirits partly Good and partly Evil, which is named THEURGIA-GOËTIA, all Aërial Spirits.

(3) THE THIRD PART is a Book governing the Planetary Houses, and what Spirits belong to every Degree of the Signs, and Planets in the Signs. Called the PAULINE ART.

(4) THE FOURTH PART is a Book called the ALMADEL OF SOLOMON, which contains Twenty Chief Spirits who govern the Four Altitudes, or the 360 Degrees of the Zodiac.

are Good, and to be sought for by Divine seeking, etc., and are called THEURGIA.

the ART PAULINE and the ART ALMADEL, do relate unto Good Spirits alone, whose knowledge is to be obtained through seeking unto the Divine. These two Books be also classed together under the Name of the First and Second Parts of the Book THEURGIA OF SOLOMON.

are Good, and are called THEURGIA, and are to be sought for by Divine seeking, etc.

These two last Orders of Spirits are Good, and called THEURGIA, and are to be sought after by Divine seeking.

(5) THE FIFTH PART is a Book of Orations and Prayers that Wise Solomon used upon the Altar in the Temple. The which is called ARS NOVA, which was revealed unto Solomon by that Holy Angel of God called MICHAEL; and he also received many brief Notes written with the Finger of God, which were declared to him by the said Angel with Claps of Thunder; without which Notes King Solomon had never obtained his great knowledge, for by them in a short time he knew all Arts and Sciences both Good and Bad: from these Notes it is called the NOTARY ART, etc.

(5) THE FIFTH BOOK of the Lemegeton is one of Prayers and Orations. The which Solomon the Wise did use upon the Altar in the Temple. And the titles hereof be ARS NOVA, the NEW ART, and ARS NOTARIA, the NOTARY ART. The which was revealed unto him by MICHAEL, that Holy Angel of God, in thunder and in lightning, and he further did receive by the aforesaid Angel certain Notes written by the Hand of God, without the which that Great King had never attained unto his great Wisdom, for thus he knew all things and all Sciences and Arts whether Good or Evil.

(5) THE FIFTH PART is a Book of Orations and Prayers which Wise Solomon did use upon the Altar in the Temple. The which is called ARS NOVA, the which was revealed to Solomon by that Holy Angel of God called Michael; and he also received many brief Notes written with the Finger of God, which were declared to him by the said Angel with Claps of Thunder; without which Notes King Solomon had never obtained his Great Wisdom, for by them in short time he gained Knowledge of all Arts and Sciences both Good and Bad; from these Notes it is called the NOTARY ART, etc.

These Most Sacred Mysteries were revealed unto Solomon.

Now in this Book LEMEGETON is contained the whole Art of King Solomon. And although there be many other Books that are said to be his, yet none is to be compared hereunto, for this containeth them all.

Though there be titles with several other Names of the Book, as THE BOOK HELISOL, which is the very same with this last Book of LEMEGETON called ARS NOVA or ARS NOTARIA, etc.

These Books were first found in the Chaldee and Hebrew Tongues at Jerusalem by a Jewish Rabbi; and by him put into the Greek language and thence into the Latin, as it is said.[1]

---

[1] The first only of these five books is here published: the astral opposition incidental to the publication of any magical writing is not to be blamed for this; but the engorgement of the translator in a matter of other import, as previously hinted. The true life of this man and his associates, with a veridic account of their researches into magical arts, *etc.*, may be looked for in my forthcoming volume:

"History of the Order of the Golden Dawn."—ED.

SHEMHAMPHORASH

(1.) BAEL. — The First Principal Spirit is a King ruling in the East, called Bael. He maketh thee to go Invisible. He ruleth over 66 Legions of Infernal Spirits. He appeareth in divers shapes, sometimes like a Cat, sometimes like a Toad, and sometimes like a Man, and sometimes all these forms at once. He speaketh hoarsely. This is his character which is used to be worn as a Lamen before him who calleth him forth, or else he will not do thee homage.[1]

Figure 5.
The Seal of Bael.

Figure 6.
Bael, as drawn
by Crowley.

Figure 7. Bael.

---

[1] I am not responsible for this ultra-Arian confusion of persons.—ED.

Figure 8.
The Seal of Agares.

(2.) AGARES. — The Second Spirit is a Duke called Agreas, or Agares. He is under the Power of the East, and cometh up in the form of an old fair Man, riding upon a Crocodile, carrying a Goshawk upon his fist, and yet mild in appearance. He maketh them to run that stand still, and bringeth back runaways. He teaches all Languages or Tongues presently. He hath power also to destroy Dignities both Spiritual and Temporal, and causeth Earthquakes. He was of the Order of Virtues. He hath under his government 31 Legions of Spirits. And this is his Seal or Character which thou shalt wear as a Lamen before thee.

Figure 9.
Agares, as drawn
by Crowley.

Figure 10. Agares.

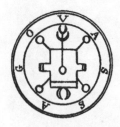

Figure 11.
The Seal of Vassago.

(3.) VASSAGO. — The Third Spirit is a Mighty Prince, being of the same nature as Agares. He is called Vassago. This Spirit is of a Good Nature, and his office is to declare things Past and to Come, and to discover all things Hid or Lost. And he governeth 26 Legions of Spirits, and this is his Seal.

(4.) SAMIGINA, or GAMIGIN.—The Fourth Spirit
is Samigina, a Great Marquis. He appeareth in
the form of a little Horse or Ass, and then into
Human shape doth he change himself at the
request of the Master. He speaketh with a hoarse
voice. He ruleth over 30 Legions of Inferiors. He
teaches all Liberal Sciences, and giveth account of
Dead Souls that died in sin. And his Seal is this,
which is to be worn before the Magician when he
is Invocator, etc.

Figure 12.
The Seal of Samigina.

Figure 13.
Samigina, as drawn
by Crowley.

(5.) MARBAS.—The Fifth Spirit is Marbas. He is
a Great President, and appeareth at first in the
form of a Great Lion, but afterwards, at the
request of the Master, he putteth on Human
Shape. He answereth truly of things Hidden or
Secret. He causeth Diseases and cureth them.
Again, he giveth great Wisdom and Knowledge in
Mechanical Arts; and can change men into other
shapes. He governeth 36 Legions of Spirits. And
his Seal is this, which is to be worn as aforesaid.

Figure 14.
The Seal of Marbas.

(6.) VALEFOR.—The Sixth Spirit is Valefor. He is a mighty Duke, and appeareth in the shape of a Lion with an Ass's Head, bellowing. He is a good Familiar, but tempteth them he is a familiar of to steal. He governeth 10 Legions of Spirits. His Seal is this, which is to be worn, whether thou wilt have him for a Familiar, or not.

Figure 15.
The Seal of Valefor.

Figure 16.
The Seal of Amon.

(7.) AMON.—The Seventh Spirit is Amon. He is a Marquis great in power, and most stern. He appeareth like a Wolf with a Serpent's tail, vomiting out of his mouth flames of fire; but at the command of the Magician he putteth on the shape of a Man with Dog's teeth beset in a head like a Raven; or else like a Man with a Raven's head (simply). He telleth all things Past and to Come. He procureth feuds and reconcileth controversies between friends. He governeth 40 Legions of Spirits. His Seal is this which is to be worn as aforesaid, etc.

Figure 17.
Amon, as drawn by
Crowley.

Figure 18. Amon.

(8.) BARBATOS.—The Eighth Spirit is Barbatos. He is a Great Duke, and appeareth when the Sun is in Sagittary, with four noble Kings and their companies of great troops. He giveth understanding of the singing of Birds, and of the Voices of other creatures, such as the barking of Dogs. He breaketh the Hidden Treasures open that have been laid by the Enchantments of Magicians. He is of the Order of Virtues, of which some part he retaineth still; and he knoweth all things Past, and to Come, and conciliateth Friends and those that be in Power. He ruleth over 30 Legions of Spirits. His Seal of Obedience is this, the which wear before thee as aforesaid.

Figure 19.
The Seal of Barbatos.

Figure 20. Barbatos.

Figure 21.
The Seal of Paimon (1).

(9.) PAIMON. — The Ninth Spirit in this Order is Paimon, a Great King, and very obedient unto LUCIFER. He appeareth in the form of a Man sitting upon a Dromedary with a Crown most glorious upon his head. There

Figure 22.
The Seal of Paimon (2).

goeth before him also an Host of Spirits, like Men with Trumpets and well sounding Cymbals, and all other sorts of Musical Instruments. He hath a great Voice, and roareth at his first coming, and his speech is such that the Magician cannot well understand unless he can compel him. This Spirit can teach all Arts and Sciences, and other secret things. He can discover unto thee what the Earth is, and what holdeth it up in the Waters; and what Mind is, and where it is; or any other thing thou mayest desire to know. He giveth Dignity, and confirmeth the same. He bindeth or maketh any man subject unto the Magician if he so desire it. He giveth good Familiars, and such as can teach all Arts. He is to be observed towards the West. He is of the Order of Dominations.[1] He hath under him 200 Legions of Spirits, and part of them are of the Order of Angels, and the other part of Potentates. Now if thou callest this Spirit Paimon alone, thou must make him some offering; and there will attend him two Kings called Labal and Abalim, and also other Spirits who be of the Order of Potentates in his Host, and 25 Legions. And those Spirits which be subject unto them are not always with them unless the Magician do compel them. His Character is this which must be worn as a Lamen before thee, etc.

Figure 23. Paimon.

---

[1] Or Dominions, as they are usually termed.

(10.) BUER.—The Tenth Spirit is Buer, a Great
President. He appeareth in Sagittary, and that is
his shape when the Sun is there.[1] He teaches Philosophy, both Moral and Natural, and the Logic
Art, and also the Virtues of all Herbs and Plants.
He healeth all distempers in man, and giveth
good Familiars. He governeth 50 Legions of Spirits, and his Character of obedience is this, which
thou must wear when thou callest him forth unto
appearance.

Figure 24.
The Seal of Buer.

Figure 25. Buer.

(11.) GUSION.—The Eleventh Spirit in order is a
great and strong Duke, called Gusion. He appeareth like a Xenopilus. He telleth all things, Past,
Present, and to Come, and showeth the meaning
and resolution of all questions thou mayest ask.
He conciliateth and reconcileth friendships, and
giveth Honour and Dignity unto any. He ruleth
over 40 Legions of Spirits. His Seal is this, the
which wear thou as aforesaid.

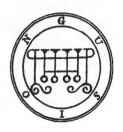

Figure 26.
The Seal of Gusion.

---

[1] (I think he can only be invoked at this time. ר ר ר .)

(12.) Sitri. — The Twelfth Spirit is Sitri. He is a Great Prince, and appeareth at first with a Leopard's head and the Wings of a Gryphon, but after the command of the Master of the Exorcism he putteth on Human shape, and that very beautiful. He enflameth men with Women's love, and Women with Men's love; and causeth them also to show themselves naked if it be desired. He governeth 60 Legions of Spirits. His Seal is this, to be worn as a Lamen before thee, etc.

Figure 27.
The Seal of Sitri.

Figure 28.
The Seal of Beleth (1).

(13.) Beleth. — The Thirteenth Spirit is called Beleth (or Bileth, or Bilet). He is a mighty King and terrible. He rideth on a pale horse with trumpets and other kinds of musical instruments playing before him. He is very furious at his first

Figure 29.
The Seal of Beleth (2).

appearance, that is, while the Exorcist layeth his courage; for to do this he must hold a Hazel Wand in his hand, striking it out towards the South and East Quarters, make a triangle, △, without the Circle, and then command him into it by the Bonds and Charges of Spirits as hereafter followeth. And if he doth not enter into the triangle, △, at your threats, rehearse the Bonds and Charms before him, and then he will yield Obedience and come into it, and do what he is commanded by the Exorcist. Yet he must receive him courteously because he is a Great King, and do homage unto him, as the Kings and Princes do that attend upon him. And thou must have always a Silver Ring on the middle finger of the left hand held against thy face,[1] as they do yet before Amaymon. This Great King Beleth causeth all the love that may be, both of Men and of Women, until the Master Exorcist hath had his desire fulfilled. He is of the Order of Powers, and he governeth 85 Legions of Spirits. His Noble Seal is this, which is to be worn before thee at working.

---

[1] To protect him from the flaming breath of the enraged Spirit; the design is given at the end of the instructions for the Magical Circle, etc., later on in the *Goetia*. [See p. 74.]

Figure 30.
The Seal of Leraje (1).

Figure 31.
The Seal of Leraje (2).

(14.) LERAJE, OR LERAIKHA. — The Fourteenth Spirit is called Leraje (or Leraie). He is a Marquis Great in Power, showing himself in the likeness of an Archer clad in Green, and carrying a Bow and Quiver. He causeth all great Battles and Contests; and maketh wounds to putrefy that are made with Arrows by Archers. This belongeth unto Sagittary. He governeth 30 Legions of Spirits, and this is his Seal, etc.

Figure 32.
The Seal of Eligos.

(15.) ELIGOS.—The Fifteenth Spirit in Order is Eligos, a Great Duke, and appeareth in the form of a goodly Knight, carrying a Lance, an Ensign, and a Serpent. He discovereth hidden things, and knoweth things to come; and of Wars, and how the Soldiers will or shall meet. He causeth the Love of Lords and Great Persons. He governeth 60 Legions of Spirits. His Seal is this, etc.

(16.) ZEPAR.—The Sixteenth Spirit is Zepar. He is a Great Duke, and appeareth in Red Apparel and Armour, like a Soldier. His office is to cause Women to love Men, and to bring them together in love. He also maketh them barren. He governeth 26 Legions of Inferior Spirits, and his Seal is this, which he obeyeth when he seeth it.

Figure 33.
The Seal of Zepar.

Figure 34.
The Seal of Botis.

(17.) BOTIS. —The Seventeenth Spirit is Botis, a Great President, and an Earl. He appeareth at the first show in the form of an ugly Viper, then at the command of the Magician he putteth on a Human shape with Great Teeth, and two Horns, carrying a bright and sharp Sword in his hand. He telleth all things Past, and to Come, and reconcileth Friends and Foes. He ruleth over 60 Legions of Spirits, and this is his Seal, etc.

Figure 35.
The Seal of Bathin (1).

Figure 36.
The Seal of Bathin (2).

(18.) BATHIN. — The Eighteenth Spirit is Bathin. He is a Mighty and Strong Duke, and appeareth like a Strong Man with the tail of a Serpent, sitting upon a Pale-coloured (Horse?).[1] He knoweth the Virtues of Herbs and Precious Stones, and can transport men suddenly from one country to another. He ruleth over 30 Legions of Spirits. His Seal is this which is to be worn as aforesaid.

(19.) SALLOS.—The Nineteenth Spirit is Sallos (or Saleos). He is a Great and Mighty Duke, and appeareth in the form of a gallant Soldier riding on a Crocodile, with a Ducal Crown on his head, but peaceably. He causeth the Love of Women to Men, and of Men to Women; and governeth 30 Legions of Spirits. His Seal is this, etc.

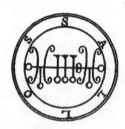

Figure 37.
The Seal of Sallos.

Figure 38. Sallos.

---

[1] In some of the older Codices this word is left out, in others it is indistinct, but appears to be "horse," so I have put the word horse within [parentheses] above. — TRANS. {The Quartos have "ass."—ED.}

(20.) PURSON.—The Twentieth Spirit is Purson, a Great King. His appearing is comely, like a Man with a Lion's face, carrying a cruel Viper in his hand, and riding upon a Bear. Going before him are many Trumpets sounding. He knoweth all things hidden, and can discover Treasure, and tell all things Past, Present, and to Come. He can take a Body either Human or Aërial, and answereth truly of all Earthly things both Secret and Divine,

Figure 39.
The Seal of Purson.

and of the Creation of the World. He bringeth forth good Familiars, and under his Government there be 22 Legions of Spirits, partly of the Order of Virtues and partly of the Order of Thrones. His Mark, Seal, or Character is this, unto the which he oweth obedience, and which thou shalt wear in time of action, etc.

Figure 40. Purson.

(21.) MARAX. — The Twenty-first Spirit is Marax.[1] He is a Great Earl and President. He appeareth like a great Bull with a Man's face. His office is to make Men very knowing in Astronomy, and all other Liberal Sciences; also he can give good Familiars, and wise, knowing the virtues of Herbs and Stones which be precious. He governeth 30 Legions of Spirits, and his Seal is this, which must be made and worn as aforesaid, etc.

Figure 41.
The Seal of Marax.

---

[1] In some Codices written Morax, but I consider the above the correct orthography.

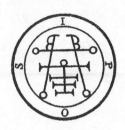

Figure 42.
The Seal of Ipos.

(22.) IPOS.—The Twenty-second Spirit is Ipos. He is an Earl, and a Mighty Prince, and appeareth in the form of an Angel with a Lion's Head, and a Goose's Foot, and Hare's Tail. He knoweth all things Past, Present, and to Come. He maketh men witty and bold. He governeth 36 Legions of Spirits. His Seal is this, which thou shalt wear, etc.

Figure 43. Ipos.

(23.) AIM.—The Twenty-third Spirit is Aim. He is a Great Strong Duke. He appeareth in the form of a very handsome Man in body, but with three Heads; the first, like a Serpent, the second like a Man having two Stars on his Forehead, the third like a Calf. He rideth on a Viper, carrying a Firebrand in his Hand, wherewith he setteth cities, castles, and great Places, on fire. He maketh thee witty in all manner of ways, and giveth true answers unto private matters. He governeth 26 Legions of Inferior Spirits; and his Seal is this, which wear thou as aforesaid, etc.

Figure 44.
The Seal of Aim.

Figure 45.
The Seal of Naberius.

(24.) NABERIUS.—The Twenty-fourth Spirit is Naberius. He is a most valiant Marquis, and showeth [himself] in the form of a Black Crane fluttering about the Circle, and when he speaketh it is with a hoarse voice. He maketh men cunning in all Arts and Sciences, but especially in the Art of Rhetoric. He restoreth lost Dignities and Honours. He governeth 19 Legions of Spirits. His Seal is this, which is to be worn, etc.

(25.) GLASYA-LABOLAS. — The Twenty-fifth Spirit is Glasya-Labolas. He is a Mighty President and Earl, and showeth himself in the form of a Dog with Wings like a Gryphon. He teacheth all Arts and Sciences in an instant, and is an Author of Bloodshed and Manslaughter. He teacheth all things Past, and to Come. If desired he causeth the love both of Friends and of Foes. He can make a Man to go Invisible. And he hath under his command 36 Legions of Spirits. His Seal is this, to be, etc.

Figure 46.
The Seal of Glasya-
Labolas.

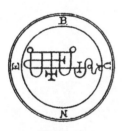

Figure 47.
The Seal of Bune (1).

(26.) BUNE, or BIMÉ.—The Twenty-sixth Spirit is Buné (or Bim). He is a Strong, Great and Mighty Duke. He appeareth in the form of a Dragon with three heads, one like a Dog, one like a Gryphon, and one like a Man. He speaketh with a

Figure 48.
The Seal of Bune (2).

high and comely Voice. He changeth the Place of the Dead, and causeth the Spirits which be under him to gather together upon your Sepulchres. He giveth Riches unto a Man, and maketh him Wise and Eloquent. He giveth true Answers unto Demands. And he governeth 30 Legions of Spirits. His Seal is this, unto the which he oweth Obedience. He hath another Seal (which is the first of these,[1] but the last is the best).[2]

---

[1] Figure 47.
[2] Figure 48.

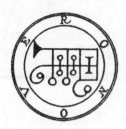

Figure 49.
The Seal of Ronové.

(27.) RONOVÉ. — The Twenty-seventh Spirit is Ronové. He appeareth in the Form of a Monster. He teacheth the Art of Rhetoric very well, and giveth Good Servants, Knowledge of Tongues, and Favours with Friends or Foes. He is a Marquis and Great Earl; and there be under his command 19 Legions of Spirits. His Seal is this, etc.

Figure 50. Ronové.

Figure 51.
The Seal of Berith.

(28.) BERITH. — The Twenty-eighth Spirit in Order, as Solomon bound them, is named Berith. He is a Mighty, Great, and Terrible Duke. He hath two other Names given unto him by men of later times, viz.: BEALE, or BEAL, and BOFRY or BOLFRY. He appeareth in the Form of a Soldier with Red Clothing, riding upon a Red Horse, and having a Crown of Gold upon his head. He giveth true answers, Past, Present, and to Come.[1] Thou must make use of a Ring in calling him forth, as is before spoken of regarding Beleth.[2] He can turn all metals into Gold. He can give Dignities, and can confirm them unto Man. He speaketh with a very clear and subtle Voice. He is a Great Liar, and not to be trusted unto. He governeth 26 Legions of Spirits. His Seal is this, etc.

---

[1] This hardly agrees with the statement that he is a great liar, and not to be trusted.
[2] See *ante*, Spirit No. 13.

Figure 52. Berith.

(29.) ASTAROTH. — The Twenty-ninth Spirit is Astaroth. He is a Mighty, Strong Duke, and appeareth in the Form of an hurtful Angel riding on an Infernal Beast like a Dragon, and carrying in his right hand a Viper. Thou must in no wise let him approach too near unto thee, lest he do thee damage by his Noisome Breath. Wherefore the Magician must hold the Magical Ring near his face, and that will defend him. He giveth true answers of things Past, Present, and to Come, and can discover all Secrets. He will declare wittingly how the Spirits fell, if desired, and the reason of his own fall. He can make men wonderfully knowing in all Liberal Sciences. He ruleth 40 Legions of Spirits. His Seal is this, which wear thou as a Lamen before thee, or else he will not appear nor yet obey thee, etc.

*Figure 53.
The Seal of Astaroth.*

Figure 54. Astaroth.

(30.) FORNEUS.—The Thirtieth Spirit is Forneus. He is a Mighty and Great Marquis, and appeareth in the Form of a Great Sea-Monster. He teacheth, and maketh men wonderfully knowing in the Art of Rhetoric. He causeth men to have a Good Name, and to have the knowledge and understanding of Tongues. He maketh one to be beloved of his Foes as well as of his Friends. He governeth 29 Legions of Spirits, partly of the Order of Thrones, and partly of that of Angels. His Seal is this, which wear thou, etc.

Figure 55.
The Seal of Forneus.

Figure 56.
The Seal of Foras.

(31.) FŌRAS. — The Thirty-first Spirit is Foras. He is a Mighty President, and appeareth in the Form of a Strong Man in Human Shape.[1] He can give the understanding to Men how they may know the Virtues of all Herbs and Precious Stones. He teacheth the Arts of Logic and Ethics in all their parts. If desired he maketh men invisible,[2] and to live long, and to be eloquent. He can discover Treasures and recover things Lost. He ruleth over 29 Legions of Spirits, and his Seal is this, which wear thou, etc.

Figure 57.
Foras, as drawn by Crowley.

---

[1] (Distinguish thus from Sandow. [?])

[2] One or two Codices have "invincible," but "invisible" is given in the majority. Yet the form of appearance of Foras as a strong man might warrant the former, though from the nature of his offices the invincibility would probably be rather on the mental than on the physical plane.

(32.) ASMODAY.—The Thirty-second Spirit is
Asmoday, or Asmodai. He is a Great King,
Strong, and Powerful. He appeareth with Three
Heads, whereof the first is like a Bull, the second
like a Man, and the third like a Ram; he hath also
the tail of a Serpent, and from his mouth issue
Flames of Fire. His Feet are webbed like those of
a Goose. He sitteth upon an Infernal Dragon, and
beareth in his hand a Lance with a Banner. He is
first and choicest under the Power of AMAYMON,

Figure 58.
The Seal of Asmoday.

he goeth before all other. When the Exorcist hath a mind to call him,
let it be abroad, and let him stand on his feet all the time of action, with
his Cap or Head-dress off; for if it be on, AMAYMON will deceive him
and call all his actions to be bewrayed. But as soon as the Exorcist
seeth Asmoday in the shape aforesaid, he shall call him by his Name,
saying: "Art thou Asmoday?" and he will not deny it, and by-and-by
he will bow down unto the ground. He giveth the Ring of Virtues; he
teacheth the Arts of Arithmetic, Astronomy, Geometry, and all handicrafts absolutely. He giveth true and full answers unto thy demands.
He maketh one Invincible. He showeth the place where Treasures lie,
and guardeth it. He, amongst the Legions of AMAYMON governeth 72
Legions of Spirits Inferior. His Seal is this which thou must wear as a
Lamen upon thy breast, etc.

Figure 59. Asmoday.

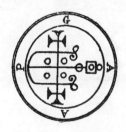

Figure 60.
The Seal of Gäap.

(33.) GÄAP.—The Thirty-third Spirit is Gäap. He is a Great President and a Mighty Prince. He appeareth when the Sun is in some of the Southern Signs, in a Human Shape, going before Four Great and Mighty Kings, as if he were a Guide to conduct them along on their way. His Office is to make men Insensible or Ignorant; as also in Philosophy to make them Knowing, and in all the Liberal Sciences. He can cause Love or Hatred, also he can teach thee to consecrate those things that belong to the Dominion of Amaymon his King. He can deliver Familiars out of the Custody of other Magicians, and answereth truly and perfectly of things Past, Present and to Come. He can carry and re-carry men very speedily from one Kingdom to another, at the Will and Pleasure of the Exorcist. He ruleth over 66 Legions of Spirits, and he was of the Order of Potentates. His Seal is this to be made and to be worn as aforesaid, etc.

Figure 61. Gäap.

(34.) FURFUR.—The Thirty-fourth Spirit is Furfur. He is a Great and Mighty Earl, appearing in the Form of an Hart with a Fiery Tail. He never speaketh truth unless he be compelled, or brought up within a triangle, △. Being therein, he will take upon himself the Form of an Angel. Being bidden, he speaketh with a hoarse voice. Also he will wittingly urge Love between Man and Woman. He can raise Lightnings and Thunders, Blasts, and Great Tempestuous Storms. And he giveth True Answers both of Things Secret and Divine, if commanded. He ruleth over 26 Legions of Spirits. And his Seal is this, etc.

Figure 63.
The Seal of Furfur.

Figure 62.
Furfur, as drawn by
Crowley.

Figure 64. Furfur.

(35.) MARCHOSIAS.—The Thirty-fifth Spirit is Marchosias. He is a Great and Mighty Marquis, appearing at first in the Form of a Wolf [1] having Gryphon's Wings, and a Serpent's Tail, and Vomiting Fire out of his mouth. But after a time, at the command of the Exorcist he putteth on the Shape of a Man. And he is a strong fighter. He was of the Order of Dominations. He governeth 30 Legions of Spirits. He told his Chief, who was Solomon, that after 1,200 years he had hopes to return unto the Seventh Throne. And his Seal is this, to be made and worn as a Lamen, etc.

Figure 65.
The Seal of
Marchosias.

Figure 66. Marchosias.

---

[1] In one Codex of the seventeenth century, very badly written, it might be read "Ox" instead of "Wolf."—TRANS. {For me he appeared always like an ox, and very dazed.—ED.}

Figure 67. Stolas.

*Figure 68.
The Seal of Stolas.*

(36.) STOLAS, or STOLOS. — The Thirty-sixth Spirit is Stolas, or Stolos. He is a Great and Powerful Prince, appearing in the Shape of a Mighty Raven at first before the Exorcist; but after he taketh the image of a Man. He teacheth the Art of Astronomy, and the Virtues of Herbs and Precious Stones. He governeth 26 Legions of Spirits; and his Seal is this, which is, etc.

*Figure 69.
The Seal of Phenex.*

(37.) PHENEX. — The Thirty-seventh Spirit is Phenex (or Pheynix). He is a Great Marquis, and appeareth like the Bird Phœnix, having the Voice of a Child. He singeth many sweet notes before the Exorcist, which he must not regard, but by-and-by he must bid him put on Human Shape. Then will he speak marvellously of all wonderful Sciences if required. He is a Poet, good and excellent. And he will be willing to perform thy requests. He hath hopes also to return to the Seventh Throne after 1,200 years more, as he said unto Solomon. He governeth 20 Legions of Spirits. And his Seal is this, which wear thou, etc.

(38.) Halphas, or Malthus. — The Thirty-eighth Spirit is Halphas, or Malthus (or Malthas). He is a Great Earl, and appeareth in the Form of a Stock-Dove. He speaketh with a hoarse Voice. His Office is to build up Towers, and to furnish them with Ammunition and Weapons, and to send Men-of-War[1] to places appointed. He ruleth over 26 Legions of Spirits, and his Seal is this, etc.[2]

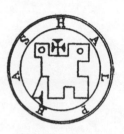

Figure 70.
The Seal of Halphas.

Figure 71.
The Seal of Malphas.

(39.) Malphas. — The Thirty-ninth Spirit is Malphas. He appeareth at first like a Crow, but after he will put on Human Shape at the request of the Exorcist, and speak with a hoarse Voice. He is a Mighty President and Powerful. He can build Houses and High Towers, and can bring to thy Knowledge Enemies' Desires and Thoughts, and that which they have done. He giveth Good Familiars. If thou makest a Sacrifice unto him he will receive it kindly and willingly, but he will deceive him that doth it. He governeth 40 Legions of Spirits, and his Seal is this, etc.

Figure 72.
Malphas.

---

[1] Or Warriors, or Men-at-Arms.

[2] But Malthus is certainly in heaven. See *Prometheus Unbound*, Introduction by P. B. Shelley, a necromancer of note, as shown by the references in his "Hymn to Intellectual Beauty."—Ed.

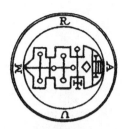

Figure 73.
The Seal of Räum.

(40.) RÄUM.—The Fortieth Spirit is Räum. He is a Great Earl; and appeareth at first in the Form of a Crow, but after the Command of the Exorcist he putteth on Human Shape. His office is to steal Treasures out [of] King's Houses, and to carry it whither he is commanded, and to destroy Cities and Dignities of Men, and to tell all things, Past, and what Is, and what Will Be; and to cause Love between Friends and Foes. He was of the Order of Thrones. He governeth 30 Legions of Spirits; and his Seal is this, which wear thou as aforesaid.

(41.) FOCALOR. — The Forty-first Spirit is Focalor, or Forcalor, or Furcalor. He is a Mighty Duke and Strong. He appeareth in the Form of a Man with Gryphon's Wings. His office is to slay Men, and to drown them in the Waters, and to overthrow Ships of War, for he hath Power over both Winds and Seas; but he will not hurt any man or thing if he be commanded to the contrary by the Exorcist. He also hath hopes to return to the Seventh Throne after 1,000 years. He governeth 30[1] Legions of Spirits, and his Seal is this, etc.

Figure 74.
The Seal of Focalor.

---

[1] Three is given instead of 30 in several Codices; but 30 is probably the more correct.

Figure 75.
The Seal of Vepar (1)

Figure 76.
The Seal of Vepar (2)

(42.) Vepar. — The Forty-second Spirit is Vepar, or Vephar. He is a Duke Great and Strong, and appeareth like a Mermaid. His office is to govern the Waters, and to guide Ships laden with Arms, Armour, and Ammunition, etc., thereon.[1] And at the request of the Exorcist he can cause the seas to be right stormy and to appear full of ships. Also he maketh men to die in Three Days by Putrefying Wounds or Sores, and causing Worms to breed in them. He governeth 29 Legions of Spirits, and his Seal is this, etc.

Figure 77.
Vepar, as drawn by Crowley.

(43.) Sabnock.—The Forty-third Spirit, as King Solomon commanded them into the Vessel of Brass, is called Sabnock, or Savnok. He is a Marquis, Mighty, Great and Strong, appearing in the Form of an Armed Soldier with a Lion's Head, riding on a pale-coloured horse. His office is to build high Towers, Castles and Cities, and to furnish them with Armour, etc. Also he can afflict Men for many days with Wounds and with Sores rotten and full of Worms. He giveth Good Familiars at the request of the Exorcist. He commandeth 50 Legions of Spirits; and his Seal is this, etc.

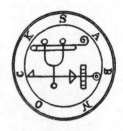

Figure 78.
The Seal of Sabnock.

---

[1] In several Codices this passage reads: "His Office is to Guide the Waters and Ships laden with Armour thereon."

(44.) SHAX.—The Forty-fourth Spirit is Shax, or
Shaz (or Shass). He is a Great Marquis and appeareth in the Form of a Stock-Dove, speaking with
a voice hoarse, but yet subtle. His Office is to take
away the Sight, Hearing, or Understanding of any
Man or Woman at the command of the Exorcist;
and to steal money out of the houses of Kings,
and to carry it again in 1,200 years. If commanded he will fetch Horses at the request of the
Exorcist, or any other thing. But he must first be

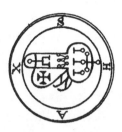

Figure 79.
The Seal of Shax.

commanded into a Triangle, △, or else he will deceive him, and tell
him many Lies. He can discover all things that are Hidden, and not
kept by Wicked Spirits. He giveth good Familiars, sometimes. He governeth 30 Legions of Spirits, and his Seal is this, etc.

Figure 80. Shax.

Figure 81.
The Seal of Viné.

(45.) VINÉ.—The Forty-fifth Spirit is Viné, or
Vinea. He is a Great King, and an Earl; and appeareth in the Form of a Lion,[1] riding upon a Black
Horse, and bearing a Viper in his hand. His Office
is to discover Things Hidden, Witches, Wizards,
and Things Present, Past, and to Come. He, at the
command of the Exorcist will build Towers, overthrow Great Stone Walls, and make the Waters
rough with Storms. He governeth 36 Legions of
Spirits. And his Seal is this, which wear thou, as aforesaid, etc.

---

[1] Or "with the Head of a Lion," or "having a Lion's Head," in some Codices.

(46.) BIFRONS.—The Forty-sixth Spirit is called Bifrons, or Bifröus, or Bifrovs. He is an Earl, and appeareth in the Form of a Monster; but after a while, at the Command of the Exorcist, he putteth on the shape of a Man. His Office is to make one knowing in Astrology, Geometry, and other Arts and Sciences. He teacheth the Virtues of Precious Stones and Woods. He changeth Dead Bodies, and putteth them in another place; also he lighteth seeming Candles upon the Graves of the

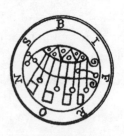

Figure 82.
The Seal of Bifrons.

Dead. He hath under his Command 6 [1] Legions of Spirits. His Seal is this, which he will own and submit unto, etc.

Figure 83.
The Seal of Uvall (1).

(47.) UVALL, VUAL, or VOVAL. — The Forty-seventh Spirit is Uvall, or Vual, or Voval. He is a Duke, Great, Mighty, and Strong; and appeareth in the Form of a Mighty Dromedary at the first, but after a while at the Command of the Exorcist he putteth on Human Shape, and speaketh the Egyptian Tongue, but not perfectly. [2] His Office is to procure the Love of Women, and to tell Things Past, Present, and to Come. He also procureth Friendship between Friends and Foes. He was of the Order of Potestates or Powers. He governeth 37 Legions of Spirits, and his Seal is this, to be made and worn before thee, etc.

Figure 84.
The Seal of Uvall (2).

---

[1] Should probably be 60 instead of 6.
[2] He can nowadays converse in sound though colloquial Coptic.—ED.

Figure 85. Uvall.

(48.) HAAGENTI.—The Forty-eighth Spirit is Haagenti. He is a President, appearing in the Form of a Mighty Bull with Gryphon's Wings. This is at first, but after, at the Command of the Exorcist he putteth on Human Shape. His Office is to make Men wise, and to instruct them in divers things; also to Transmute all Metals into Gold; and to change Wine into Water, and Water into Wine. He governeth 33 Legions of Spirits, and his Seal is this, etc.

Figure 86.
The Seal of Haagenti.

Figure 87.
The Seal of Crocell.

(49.) CROCELL.—The Forty-ninth Spirit is Crocell, or Crokel. He appeareth in the Form of an Angel. He is a Duke Great and Strong, speaking something Mystically of Hidden Things. He teacheth the Art of Geometry and the Liberal Sciences. He, at the Command of the Exorcist, will produce Great Noises like the Rushings of many Waters, although there be none. He warmeth Waters, and discovereth Baths. He was of the Order of Potestates, or Powers, before his fall, as he declared unto the King Solomon. He governeth 48 Legions of Spirits. His Seal is this, the which wear thou as aforesaid.

Figure 88.
The Seal of Furcas.

(50.) Furcas.—The Fiftieth Spirit is Furcas. He is a Knight, and appeareth in the Form of a Cruel Old Man with a long Beard and a hoary Head, riding upon a pale-coloured Horse, with a Sharp Weapon in his hand. His Office is to teach the Arts of Philosophy, Astrology, Rhetoric, Logic, Cheiromancy, and Pyromancy, in all their parts, and perfectly. He hath under his Power 20 Legions of Spirits. His Seal, or Mark, is thus made, etc.

Figure 89.
Furcas.

(51.) Balam. —The Fifty-first Spirit is Balam or Balaam. He is a Terrible, Great, and Powerful King. He appeareth with three Heads: the first is like that of a Bull; the second is like that of a Man; the third is like that of a Ram. He hath the Tail of a Serpent, and Flaming Eyes. He rideth upon a furious Bear, and carrieth a Goshawk upon his Fist. He speaketh with a hoarse Voice, giving True Answers of Things Past, Present, and to Come. He maketh men to go Invisible, and also to be Witty. He governeth 40 Legions of Spirits. His Seal is this, etc.

Figure 90.
The Seal of Balam.

Figure 91. Balam.

(52.) ALLOCES. — The Fifty-second Spirit is
Alloces, or Alocas. He is a Duke, Great, Mighty,
and Strong, appearing in the Form of a Soldier[1]
riding upon a Great Horse. His Face is like that
of a Lion, very Red, and having Flaming Eyes.
His Speech is hoarse and very big.[2] His Office is
to teach the Art of Astronomy, and all the Liberal
Sciences. He bringeth unto thee Good Familiars;
also he ruleth over 36 Legions of Spirits. His Seal
is this, which, etc.

Figure 92.
The Seal of Alloces.

Figure 93. Alloces.

[1] Or Warrior.
[2] Thus expressed in the Codices.

Figure 94.
The Seal of Camio.

(53.) Camio or Caïm. — The Fifty-third Spirit is Camio, or Caïm. He is a Great President, and appeareth in the Form of the Bird called a Thrush at first, but afterwards he putteth on the Shape of a Man carrying in his Hand a Sharp Sword. He seemeth to answer in Burning Ashes, or in Coals of Fire. He is a Good Disputer. His Office is to give unto Men the Understanding of all Birds, Lowing of Bullocks, Barking of Dogs, and other Creatures; and also of the Voice of the Waters. He giveth True Answers of Things to Come. He was of the Order of Angels, but now ruleth over 30 Legions of Spirits Infernal. His Seal is this, which wear thou, etc.

Figure 95. Camio (1).

Figure 96. Camio (2).

Figure 97.
The Seal of Murmur.

(54.) MURMUR, or MURMUS. — The Fifty-fourth Spirit is called Murmur, or Murmus, or Murmux. He is a Great Duke, and an Earl; and appeareth in the Form of a Warrior riding upon a Gryphon, with a Ducal Crown upon his Head. There do go before him those his Ministers with great Trumpets sounding. His Office is to teach Philosophy perfectly, and to constrain Souls Deceased to come before the Exorcist to answer those questions which he may wish to put to them, if desired. He was partly of the Order of Thrones, and partly of that of Angels. He now ruleth 30 Legions of Spirits. And his Seal is this, etc.

(55.) OROBAS.—The Fifty-fifth Spirit is Orobas. He is a Great and Mighty Prince, appearing at first like a Horse; but after the command of the Exorcist he putteth on the Image of a Man. His Office is to discover all things Past, Present, and to Come; also to give Dignities, and Prelacies, and the Favour of Friends and of Foes. He giveth True Answers of Divinity, and of the Creation of the World. He is very faithful unto the Exorcist, and will not suffer him to be tempted of any Spirit. He governeth 20 Legions of Spirits. His Seal is this, etc.

Figure 98.
The Seal of Orobas.

Figure 99. Orobas.

Figure 100.
The Seal of Gremory.

(56.) Gremory, or Gamori.—The Fifty-sixth Spirit is Gremory, or Gamori. He is a Duke Strong and Powerful, and appeareth in the Form of a Beautiful Woman, with a Duchess's Crown tied about her waist, and riding on a Great Camel. His Office is to tell of all Things Past, Present, and to Come; and of Treasures Hid, and what they lie in; and to procure the Love of Women both Young and Old. He governeth 26 Legions of Spirits, and his Seal is this, etc.

Figure 101. Gremory.

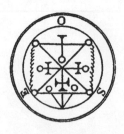

Figure 102.
The Seal of Osé.

(57.) Osé, or Voso.—The Fifty-seventh Spirit is Oso, Osé, or Voso. He is a Great President, and appeareth like a Leopard at the first, but after a little time he putteth on the Shape of a Man. His Office is to make one cunning in the Liberal Sciences, and to give True Answers of Divine and Secret Things; also to change a Man into any Shape that the Exorcist pleaseth, so that he that is so changed will not think any other thing than that he is in verity that Creature or Thing he is changed into. He governeth 3[1] Legions of Spirits, and this is his Seal, etc.

---

[1] Should probably be 30. For these 72 Great Spirits of the Book *Goetia* are all Princes and Leaders of numbers.

Figure 103.
The Seal of Amy.

(58.) AMY, or AVNAS.—The Fifty-eighth Spirit is Amy, or Avnas. He is a Great President, and appeareth at first in the Form of a Flaming Fire; but after a while he putteth on the Shape of a Man. His office is to make one Wonderful Knowing[1] in Astrology and all the Liberal Sciences. He giveth Good Familiars, and can bewray Treasure that is kept by Spirits. He governeth 36 Legions of Spirits, and his Seal is this, etc.

(59.) ORIAX, or ORIAS.—The Fifty-ninth Spirit is Oriax, or Orias. He is a Great Marquis, and appeareth in the Form of a Lion,[2] riding upon a Horse Mighty and Strong, with a Serpent's Tail;[3] and he holdeth in his Right Hand two Great Serpents hissing. His Office is to teach the Virtues of the Stars, and to know the Mansions of the Planets, and how to understand their Virtues. He also transformeth Men, and he giveth Dignities, Prelacies, and Confirmation thereof; also Favour with Friends and with Foes. He doth govern 30 Legions of Spirits; and his Seal is this, etc.

Figure 104.
The Seal of Oriax.

Figure 105.
The Seal of Vapula.

(60.) VAPULA, or NAPHULA.—The Sixtieth Spirit is Vapula, or Naphula. He is a Duke Great, Mighty, and Strong; appearing in the Form of a Lion with Gryphon's Wings. His Office is to make Men Knowing in all Handicrafts and Professions, also in Philosophy, and other Sciences. He governeth 36 Legions of Spirits, and his Seal or Character is thus made, and thou shalt wear it as aforesaid, etc.

---

[1] Thus in the actual Text.
[2] Or "with the Face of a Lion."
[3] The horse, or the Markis?—ED.

Figure 106.
The Seal of Zagan.

(61.) ZAGAN.—The Sixty-first Spirit is Zagan. He is a Great King and President, appearing at first in the Form of a Bull with Gryphon's Wings; but after a while he putteth on Human Shape. He maketh Men Witty. He can turn Wine into Water, and Blood into Wine, also Water into Wine. He can turn all Metals into Coin of the Dominion that Metal is of. He can even make Fools Wise. He governeth 33 Legions of Spirits, and his Seal is this, etc.

(62.) VOLAC, or VALAK, or VALU, or UALAC.— The Sixty-second Spirit is Volac, or Valak, or Valu. He is a President Mighty and Great, and appeareth like a Child with Angel's Wings, riding on a Two-headed Dragon. His Office is to give True Answers of Hidden Treasures, and to tell where Serpents may be seen. The which he will bring unto the Exorciser without any Force or Strength being by him employed. He governeth 38 Legions of Spirits, and his Seal is thus.

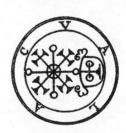

Figure 107.
The Seal of Volac.

Figure 108.
Volac.

Figure 109.
The Seal of Andras.

(63.) ANDRAS.—The Sixty-third Spirit is Andras. He is a Great Marquis, appearing in the Form of an Angel with a Head like a Black Night Raven, riding upon a strong Black Wolf, and having a Sharp and Bright Sword flourished aloft in his hand. His Office is to sow Discords. If the Exorcist have not a care, he will slay both him and his fellows. He governeth 30 Legions of Spirits, and this is his Seal, etc.

Figure 110. Andras.

(64.) HAURES, or HAURAS, or HAVRES, or FLAUROS. — The Sixty-fourth Spirit is Haures, or Hauras, or Havres, or Flauros. He is a Great Duke, and appeareth at first like a Leopard, Mighty, Terrible, and Strong, but after a while, at the Command of the Exorcist, he putteth on Human Shape with Eyes Flaming and Fiery, and a most Terrible Countenance. He giveth True Answers of all things, Present, Past, and to Come.

Figure 111.
The Seal of Haures.

But if he be not commanded into a Triangle, △, he will Lie in all these Things, and deceive and beguile the Exorcist in these things or in such and such business. He will, lastly, talk of the Creation of the World, and of Divinity, and of how he and other Spirits fell. He destroyeth and burneth up those who be the Enemies of the Exorcist should he so desire it; also he will not suffer him to be tempted by any other Spirit or otherwise. He governeth 36 Legions of Spirits, and his Seal is this, to be worn as a Lamen, etc.

Figure 112. Haures.

Figure 113. The Seal of Andrealphus.

(65.) ANDREALPHUS.—The Sixty-fifth Spirit is Andrealphus. He is a Mighty Marquis, appearing at first in the form of a Peacock, with great Noises. But after a time he putteth on Human shape. He can teach Geometry perfectly. He maketh Men very subtle therein; and in all Things pertaining unto Mensuration or Astronomy. He can transform a Man into the Likeness of a Bird. He governeth 30 Legions of Infernal Spirits, and his Seal is this, etc.

Figure 114. Andrealphus.

Figure 115.
The Seal of Cimejes.

(66.) CIMEJES, or CIMEIES, or KIMARIS.—The Sixty-sixth Spirit is Cimejes, or Cimeies, or Kimaris. He is a Marquis, Mighty, Great, Strong and Powerful, appearing like a Valiant Warrior riding upon a goodly Black Horse. He ruleth over all Spirits in the parts of Africa. His Office is to teach perfectly Grammar, Logic, Rhetoric, and to discover things Lost or Hidden, and Treasures. He governeth 20 Legions of Infernals; and his Seal is this, etc.

(67.) AMDUSIAS, or AMDUKIAS. — The Sixty-seventh Spirit is Amdusias, or Amdukias. He is a Duke Great and Strong, appearing at first like a Unicorn, but at the request of the Exorcist he standeth before him in Human Shape, causing Trumpets, and all manner of Musical Instruments to be heard, but not soon or immediately. Also he can cause Trees to bend and incline according to the Exorcist's Will. He giveth Excellent Familiars. He governeth 29 Legions of Spirits. And his Seal is this, etc.

Figure 116.
The Seal of Amdusias.

Figure 117. Amdusias.

(68.) BELIAL.—The Sixty-eighth Spirit is Belial. He is a Mighty and Powerful King, and was created next after LUCIFER. He appeareth in the Form of Two Beautiful Angels sitting in a Chariot of Fire. He speaketh with a Comely Voice, and declareth that he fell first from among the worthier sort, that were before Michael, and other Heavenly Angels. His Office is to distribute Presentations and Senatorships, etc., and to cause

Figure 118.
The Seal of Belial.

favour of Friends and of Foes. He giveth excellent Familiars, and governeth 80[1] Legions of Spirits. Note well that this King Belial must have Offerings, Sacrifices and Gifts presented unto him by the Exorcist, or else he will not give True Answers unto his Demands. But then he tarrieth not one hour in the Truth, unless he be constrained by Divine Power. And his Seal is this, which is to be worn as aforesaid, etc.

Figure 119.
The Seal of Decarabia.

(69.) DECARABIA. — The Sixty-ninth Spirit is Decarabia. He appeareth in the Form of a Star in a Pentacle, ☆, at first; but after, at the command of the Exorcist, he putteth on the Image of a Man. His Office is to discover the Virtues of Birds and Precious Stones, and to make the Similitude of all kinds of Birds to fly before the Exorcist, singing and drinking as natural Birds do. He governeth 30 Legions of Spirits, being himself a Great Marquis. And this is his Seal, which is to be worn, etc.

Figure 120.
The Seal of Seere (1).

(70.) SEERE, SEAR, or SEIR. — The Seventieth Spirit is Seere, Sear, or Seir. He is a Mighty Prince, and Powerful, under AMAYMON, King of the East. He appeareth in the Form of a Beautiful Man, riding upon a Winged Horse. His Office is to go and come; and to bring

Figure 121.
The Seal of Seere (2).

---

[1] Perhaps an error for 30.—TRANS.   The actual number is 50; at least it was in 1898.—ED. (An. XIX [1924 E.V.]   It is now 80 again—thanks greatly to my own Work.)

abundance of things to pass on a sudden, and to carry or re-carry anything whither thou wouldest have it to go, or whence thou wouldest have it from. He can pass over the whole Earth in the twinkling of an Eye. He giveth a True relation of all sorts of Theft, and of Treasure hid, and of many other things. He is of an indifferent Good Nature, and is willing to do anything which the Exorcist desireth. He governeth 26 Legions of Spirits. And this his Seal is to be worn, etc.

Figure 122.
The Seal of
Dantalion.

(71.) DANTALION.—The Seventy-first Spirit is Dantalion. He is a Duke Great and Mighty, appearing in the Form of a Man with many Countenances, all Men's and Women's Faces; and he hath a Book in his right hand. His Office is to teach all Arts and Sciences unto any; and to declare the Secret Counsels of any one; for he knoweth the Thoughts of all Men and Women, and can change them at his Will. He can cause Love, and show the Similitude of any person, and show the same by a Vision, let them be in what part of the World they Will. He governeth 36 Legions of Spirits; and this is his Seal, which wear thou, etc.

Figure 123.
The Seal of
Andromalius.

(72.) ANDROMALIUS. — The Seventy-second Spirit in Order is named Andromalius. He is an Earl, Great and Mighty, appearing in the Form of a Man holding a Great Serpent in his Hand. His Office is to bring back both a Thief, and the Goods which be stolen; and to discover all Wickedness, and Underhand Dealing; and to punish all Thieves and other Wicked People; and also to discover Treasures that be Hid. He ruleth over 36 Legions of Spirits. His Seal is this, the which wear thou as aforesaid, etc.

THESE be the 72 Mighty Kings and Princes which King Solomon Commanded into a Vessel of Brass, together with their Legions. Of whom BELIAL, BILETH, ASMODAY, and GÄAP, were Chief. And it is to be noted that Solomon did this because of their pride, for he never declared other reason why he thus bound them. And when he had thus bound them up and sealed the Vessel, he by Divine Power did chase them all into a deep Lake or Hole in Babylon. And they of Babylon, wondering to see such a thing, they did then go wholly into the Lake, to break the Vessel open, expecting to find great store of Treasure therein. But when they had broken it open, out flew the Chief Spirits immediately, with their Legions following them; and they were all restored to their former places except BELIAL, who entered into a certain Image, and thence gave answers unto those who did offer Sacrifices unto him, and did worship the Image as their God, etc.

OBSERVATIONS

FIRST, thou shalt know and observe the Moon's Age for thy working. The best days be when the Moon Luna is 2, 4, 6, 8, 10, 12, or 14 days old, as Solomon saith; and no other days be profitable. The Seals of the 72 Kings are to be made in Metals. The Chief Kings' in Sol (Gold); Marquises' in Luna (Silver); Dukes' in Venus (Copper); Prelacies' in Jupiter (Tin); Knights' in Saturn (Lead); Presidents' in Mercury (Mercury); Earls' in Venus (Copper), and Luna (Silver), alike equal, etc.

THESE 72 Kings be under the Power of AMAYMON, CORSON, ZIMIMAY or ZIMINIAR, and GÖAP, who are the Four Great Kings ruling in the Four Quarters, or Cardinal Points,[1] viz.: East, West, North, and South, and are not to be called forth except it be upon Great Occasions; but are to be Invocated and Commanded to send such or such a Spirit that is under their Power and Rule, as is shown in the following Invocations or Conjurations. And the Chief Kings may be bound from 9 till 12 o'clock at Noon, and from 3 till sunset; Marquises may be bound from 3 in the afternoon till 9 at Night, and from 9 at Night till Sunrise; Dukes may be bound from Sunrise till Noonday in Clear Weather; Prelates may be bound any hour of the Day; Knights may from Dawning of Day till Sunrise, or from 4 o'clock till Sunset; Presidents may be bound at any time, excepting Twilight, at Night, unless the King whom they are under be Invocated; and Counties or Earls any hour of the Day, so it be in Woods, or in any other places whither men resort not, or where no noise is, etc.

---

[1] These four Great Kings are usually called Oriens, or Uriens, Paymon or Paymonia, Ariton or Egyn, and Amaymon or Amaimon. By the Rabbins they are frequently entitled: Samael, Azazel, Azäel, and Mahazael.

CLASSIFIED LIST OF THE
72 CHIEF SPIRITS OF THE GOETIA,
ACCORDING TO RESPECTIVE RANK

(☉)   (Seal in Gold.) KINGS.—(1.) Bael; (9.) Paimon; (13.) Beleth; (20.) Purson; (32.) Asmoday; (45.) Viné; (51.) Balam; (61.) Zagan; (68.) Belial.

(♀)   (Seal in Copper.) DUKES.—(2.) Agares; (6.) Valefor; (8.) Barbatos; (11.) Gusion; (15.) Eligos; (16.) Zepar; (18.) Bathin; (19.) Sallos; (23.) Aim; (26.) Buné; (28.) Berith; (29.) Astaroth; (41.) Focalor; (42.) Vepar; (47.) Vual; (49.) Crocell; (52.) Alloces; (54.) Murmur; (56.) Gremory; (60.) Vapula; (64.) Haures; (67.) Amdusias; (71.) Dantalion.

(♃)   (Seal in Tin.) PRINCES and PRELATES.—(3.) Vassago; (12.) Sitri; (22.) Ipos; (33.) Gäap; (36.) Stolas; (55.) Orobas; (70.) Seere.

(☽)   (Seal in Silver.) MARQUISES.—(4.) Samigina; (7.) Amon; (14.) Lerajé; (24.) Naberius; (27.) Ronové; (30.) Forneus; (35.) Marchosias; (37.) Phenex; (43.) Sabnock; (44.) Shax; (59.) Orias; (63.) Andras; (65.) Andrealphus; (66) Cimeies; (69.) Decarabia.

(☿)   (Seal in Mercury.) PRESIDENTS.—(5.) Marbas; (10.) Buer; (17.) Botis; (21.) Marax; (25.) Glasya-Labolas; (31.) Foras; (33.) Gäap; (39.) Malphas; (48.) Häagenti; (53.) Caïm; (57.) Ose; (58.) Amy; (61.) Zagan; (62.) Valac.

(♂)   (Seal in Copper and Silver alike equal.) EARLS, or COUNTS.—(17.) Botis; (21.) Marax; (25.) Glasya-Labolas; (27.) Ronové; (34.) Furfur; (38.) Halphas; (40.) Räum; (45.) Viné; (46.) Bifrons; (72.) Andromalius.

(♄)   (Seal in Lead.) KNIGHTS.—(50.) Furcas.

NOTE.—It will be remarked that several among the above Spirits possess two titles of different ranks: e.g., (45.) Viné is both King and Earl; (25.) Glasya-Labolas is both President and Earl, etc. "Prince" and "Prelate" are apparently used as interchangeable terms. Probably the Seals of Earls should be made in Iron, and those of Presidents in mixture either of Copper and Silver, or of Silver and Mercury; as otherwise the Metal of one Planet, Mars, is excluded from the List; the Metals attributed to the Seven Planets being: to Saturn, Lead; to Jupiter, Tin; to Mars, Iron; to the Sun, Gold; to Venus, Copper; to Mercury, Mercury and mixtures of Metals, and to Luna, Silver.

NOTE

IN A manuscript codex by Dr. Rudd, which is in the British Museum, Hebrew names of these 72 Spirits are given; but it appears to me that many are manifestly incorrect in orthography. The codex in question, though beautifully written, also contains many other errors, particularly in the Sigils. Such as they are, these names in the Hebrew of Dr. Rudd are here shown.[1]

---

[1] [These have been given in the tables in an appendix beginning on p. 127.]

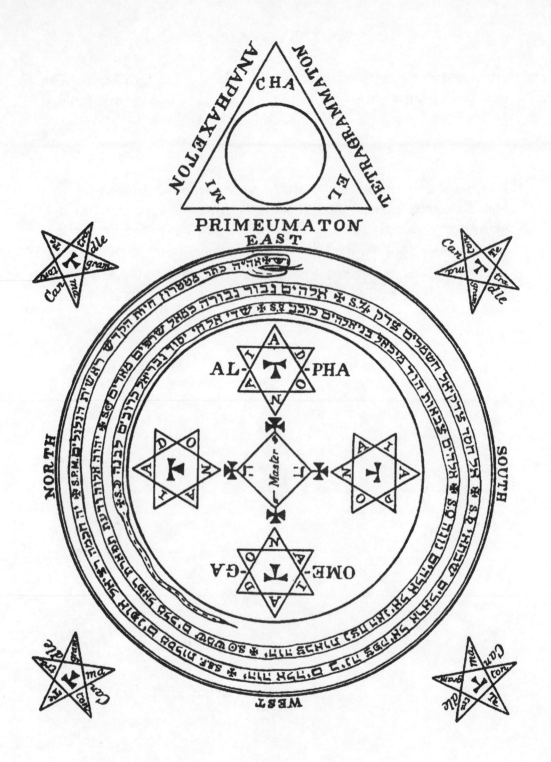

Figures 124–125. The Magical Circle and Magical Triangle.

70

THE MAGICAL REQUISITES

THE MAGICAL CIRCLE

THIS is the Form of the Magical Circle of King Solomon, the which he made that he might preserve himself therein from the malice of these Evil Spirits. [*See Figure 124 opposite.*] This Magical Circle is to be made 9 feet across, and the Divine Names are to be written round it, beginning at EHYEH, and ending at LEVANAH, Luna.

(Colours.—The space between the outer and inner circles, where the serpent is coiled, with the Hebrew names written along his body, is bright deep yellow. The square in the centre of the circle, where the word "Master" is written, is filled in with red. All names and letters are in black. In the Hexagrams the outer triangles where the letters *a, d, o, n, a, i,* appear are filled in with bright yellow, the centres, where the T-shaped crosses are, blue or green. In the Pentagrams outside the circle, the outer triangles where "Te, tra, gram, ma, ton," is written are filled in bright yellow, and the centres with the T crosses written therein are red.)[1]

THE MAGICAL TRIANGLE OF SOLOMON

THIS is the Form of the Magical Triangle, into the which Solomon did command the Evil Spirits. It is to be made at 2 feet distance from the Magical Circle and it is 3 feet across. [*See Figure 125 opposite.*] Note

---

[1] [See note on following page.]

that this triangle is to be placed toward that quarter whereunto the Spirit belongeth. And the base of the triangle is to be nearest unto the Circle, the apex pointing in the direction of the quarter of the Spirit. Observe thou also the Moon in thy working, as aforesaid, etc. Anaphaxeton is sometimes written Anepheneton.

(Colours.—Triangle outlined in black; name of Michael black on white ground; the three Names without the triangle written in red; circle in centre entirely filled in in dark green.)

---

1. The coiled serpent is only shown in one private codex, the Hebrew names being in most cases simply written round in a somewhat spiral arrangement within the double circle. It is to be remembered that Hebrew is always written from right to left, instead of from left to right like ordinary European languages. The small Maltese crosses are placed to mark the conclusion of each separate set of Hebrew names. These names are those of Deity Angels and Archangels allotted by the Qabalists to each of the 9 first Sephiroth or Divine Emanations. In English letters they run thus, beginning from the head of the serpent: ✠ Ehyeh Kether Metatron Chaioth Ha-Qadesh Rashith Ha-Galgalim S.P.M. (for "Sphere of the Primum Mobile") ✠ Iah Chokmah Ratziel Auphanim Masloth S.S.F. (for "Sphere of the Fixed Stars," or S.Z. for "Sphere of the Zodiac") ✠ Iehovah Elohim Binah Tzaphquiel Aralim Shabbathai S. (for "Sphere") of Saturn ✠ El Chesed Tzadquiel Chaschmalim Tzedeq S. of Jupiter ✠ Elohim Gibor Geburah Kamael Seraphim Madim S. of Mars ✠ Iehovah Eloah Va-Daäth Tiphereth Raphaël Malakim Shemesh S. of the Sun ✠ Iehovah Tzabaoth Netzach Haniel Elohim Nogah S. of Venus. ✠ Elohim Tzabaoth Hod Michaël Beni Elohim Kokav S. of Mercury ✠ Shaddaï El Chai Iesod Gabriel Cherubim Levanah S. of the Moon ✠.

THE HEXAGRAM OF SOLOMON

*Figure 126. The Hexagram
of Solomon.*

THIS is the Form of the Hexagram of Solomon, the figure whereof is
to be made on parchment of a calf's skin, and worn at the skirt of thy
white vestment, and covered with a cloth of fine linen white and pure,
the which is to be shown unto the Spirits when they do appear, so that
they be compelled to take human shape upon them and be obedient.

(Colours.—Circle, Hexagram, and T cross in centre outlined in
black, Maltese crosses black; the five exterior triangles of the
Hexagram where Te, tra, gram, ma, ton, is written, are filled in with
bright yellow; the T cross in centre is red, with the three little squares
therein in black. The lower exterior triangle, where the Sigil is drawn
in black,[1] is left white. The words "Tetragrammaton" and "Tau" are
in black letters; and AGLA with Alpha and Omega in red letters.)

---

[1] This sigil is frequently reversed, thus: — 𝐓 ⊢ .

THE PENTAGRAM OF SOLOMON

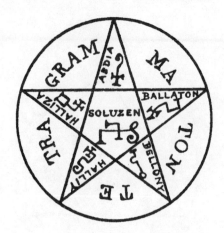

Figure 127.
The Pentagram
of Solomon.

THIS is the Form of the Pentagram of Solomon, the figure whereof is to be made in Sol or Luna (Gold or Silver), and worn upon thy breast; having the Seal of the Spirit required upon the other side thereof. It is to preserve thee from danger, and also to command the Spirits by.

(Colours.—Circle and pentagram outlined in black. Names and Sigils within Pentagram black also. "Tetragrammaton" in red letters. Ground of centre of Pentagram, where "Soluzen" is written, green. External angles of Pentagram where "Abdia," "Ballaton," "Halliza," etc., are written, blue.)

THE MAGIC RING OR DISC OF SOLOMON

Figure 128.
The Magic Ring or
Disc of Solomon.

THIS is the Form of the Magic Ring, or rather Disc, of Solomon, the figure whereof is to be made in gold or silver. It is to be held before the face of the exorcist to preserve him from the stinking sulphurous fumes and flaming breath of the Evil Spirits.

(Colour.—Bright yellow. Letters, black.)

THE VESSEL OF BRASS

Figure 129. The Vessel of Brass.

*Figure 130. The Vessel of Brass;
alternate form.*

*Figure 131.
The Seal of the Vessel.*

THIS is the Form of the Vessel of Brass wherein King Solomon did shut up the Evil Spirits, etc. (*See Figures 129 and 130.*) (Somewhat different forms are given in the various codices. The seal in Figure 131 was made in brass to cover this vessel with at the top. This history of the *djinn* shut up in the brazen vessel by King Solomon recalls the story of "The Fisherman and the Djinn" in *The Arabian Nights*. In this tale, however, there was only one *djinn* shut up in a vessel of yellow brass the which was covered at the top with a leaden seal. This *djinn* tells the fisherman that his name is Sakhr, or Sacar.)

(Colour.—Bronze. Letters.—Black on a red band.)

THE SECRET SEAL OF SOLOMON

Figure 132.
The Secret Seal
of Solomon.

THIS is the Form of the Secret Seal of Solomon, wherewith he did bind and seal up the aforesaid Spirits with their legions in the Vessel of Brass.

This seal is to be made by one that is clean both inwardly and outwardly, and that hath not defiled himself by any woman in the space of a month, but hath in prayer and fasting desired of God to forgive him all his sins, etc.

It is to be made on the day of Mars or Saturn (Tuesday or Saturday) at night at 12 o'clock, and written upon virgin parchment with the blood of a black cock that never trode hen. Note that on this night the moon must be increasing in light (i.e. going from new to full) and in the Zodiacal Sign of Virgo. And when the seal is so made thou shalt perfume it with alum, raisins dried in the sun, dates, cedar, and lignum aloes.

Also by this seal King Solomon did command all the aforesaid Spirits into the Vessel of Brass, and did seal it up with this same seal. He by it gained the love of all manner of persons, and overcame in battle, for neither weapons, nor fire, nor water could hurt him. And this privy seal was made to cover the vessel at the top withal, etc.

NOTE

FIGURES 133 to 145 inclusive are interesting as showing a marked resemblance to the central design of the Secret Seal. It will be observed that the evident desire is to represent hieroglyphically a person raising his or her hands in adoration. Nearly all are stone sepulchral steles, and the execution of them is rough and primitive in the extreme. Most are in the Musée du Louvre at Paris.

Figures 133 and 134 are from the district of Constantine and show a figure raising its arms in adoration.

In Figure 135, also from Constantine, the person bears a palm branch in the right hand.

Figs. 133–134.   *Fig. 135.*

Above is a hieroglyphic representing either the Lunar Disc or the Sun in the heavens; but more probably the former.

Fig. 136.

Fig. 137.

Figure 136 is a more complicated stele. Above is the symbol already mentioned, then comes the sign of the Pentagram, represented by a five-pointed star, towards which the person raises his or her hands. Besides the latter is a rude form of caduceus. A brief inscription follows in the Punic character. The Punic or Carthaginian language is usually considered to have been a dialect of Phœnician, and Carthage was of course a colony of Tyre. Beneath the Punic inscription is a horse's head in better drawing than the sculpture of the rest of the stele, which would seem to imply that the rudeness of the representation of the human figure is intentional. This and the following stele are also from Constantine.

In Figure 137 again, the horse is best delineated by far. In addition to the other symbols there is either a hand or a foot, for it is almost impossible to distinguish which, at the head of the stele, followed by an egg-and-tongue moulding. The figure of the person with the arms raised is treated as a pure hieroglyphic and is placed between two rude caducei. The Lunar or Solar symbol follows.

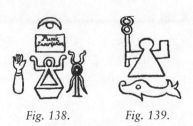

Fig. 138.   Fig. 139.

Fig. 140.

Figure 138, also from Constantine, shows the last-mentioned symbol above. The figure with the arms raised is simply a hieroglyph, and is placed between an arm and hand on the one side, and a rude caduceus on the other.

Figure 139 shows the person holding a rude caduceus in the right hand, and standing above a dolphin. This latter, as in the case of the horse in 136 and 137, is by far the best delineated.

Figure 140, this also being from Constantine, shows the usual human hieroglyph between a caduceus and a crescent.

Figure 141 is from the site of ancient Carthage. It is very rough in workmanship, and the designs are mere scratchings on the stone. The *ensemble* has the effect of an evil Sigil.

Fig. 141.

Fig. 142.

Fig. 143.   Fig. 144.

Figure 142 is also from Carthage and the various symbols appear to have become compressed into and synthesized in the form of a peculiarly evil-looking caduceus.

Figure 143 is from the decoration of a sepulchural urn found at Oldenburgh in Germany. It is remarkable as showing the same hieroglyphic human form with the crescent above; the latter in the Secret Seal of Solomon has a flattened top, and is therefore more like a bowl, and is placed across the hieroglyph.

Figure 144 is an Egyptian design which would show an analogy between the symbol and the idea of the force of the creation.

Figure 145 is a stele from Phœnicia somewhat similar to the others, except that the rudimentary caducei in Figures 137 and 141 are here replaced by two roughly drawn Ionic columns.

Fig. 145.

These last three designs are taken from the work of the Chevalier Emile Soldi-Colbert de Beaulieu, on the "*Langue Sacrée.*"[1]

Fig. 146.

In Figure 146 is given the Seal of the Spirit HALAHEL. This Spirit is said to be under the rule of BAEL, and to be of a mixed nature, partly good and partly evil, like the spirits of *Theurgia-Goetia* which follow in the second book of the *Lemegeton*.[2]

---

[1] [Emile Soldi-Colbert de Beaulieu [Emile Arthur Soldi], *La langue sacrée: la cosmoglyphie, le mystère de la création* (3 vols., Paris: Librairie A. Heymann et E. Laroux, 1897–1900).]

[2] NOTE.—I am not responsible for the accuracy of the above note.—ED.

THE OTHER
MAGICAL REQUISITES

THE other magical requisites are: a sceptre, a sword, a mitre, a cap, a long white robe of linen, and other garments for the purpose;[1] also a girdle of lion's skin three inches broad, with all the names written about it which be round the outmost part of the Magical Circle. Also perfumes, and a chafing-dish of charcoal kindled to put the fumes on, to smoke or perfume the place appointed for action; also anointing oil to anoint thy temples and thine eyes with; and fair water to wash thyself in. And in so doing, thou shalt say as David said:

THE ADORATION AT THE BATH

"THOU shalt purge me with hyssop, O Lord! and I shall be clean: Thou shalt wash me, and I shall be whiter than snow."

And at the putting on of thy garments thou shalt say:

THE ADORATION AT THE INDUING OF THE VESTMENTS

"BY the figurative mystery of these holy vestures (or of this holy vestment) I will clothe me with the armour of salvation in the strength of the Most High, ANCOR; AMACOR; AMIDES; THEODONIAS; ANITOR; that my desired end may be effected through Thy strength, O ADONAI! unto Whom the praise and glory will for ever and ever belong! Amen!"

After thou hast so done, make prayers unto God according unto thy work, as Solomon hath commanded.

---

[1] In many codices it is written "a sceptre or sword, a mitre or cap." By the "other garments" would be meant not only under-garments, but also mantles of different colours.

THE CONJURATIONS

THE CONJURATION TO CALL FORTH
ANY OF THE AFORESAID SPIRITS

I DO invoke and conjure thee, O Spirit, N.;[1] and being with power armed from the SUPREME MAJESTY, I do strongly command thee, by BERALANENSIS, BALDACHIENSIS, PAUMACHIA, and APOLOGIÆ SEDES; by the most Powerful Princes, Genii, Liachidæ, and Ministers of the Tartarean Abode; and by the Chief Prince of the Seat of Apologia in the Ninth Legion, I do invoke thee, and by invocating conjure thee. And being armed with power from the SUPREME MAJESTY, I do strongly command thee, by Him Who spake and it was done, and unto whom all creatures be obedient. Also I, being made after the image of GOD, endued with power from GOD, and created according unto His will, do exorcise thee by that most mighty and powerful name of GOD, EL, strong and wonderful; O thou Spirit N. And I command thee by Him who spake the Word and His FIAT was accomplished, and by all the names of GOD. Also by the names ADONAI, EL, ELOHIM, ELOHI, EHYEH ASHER EHYEH, ZABAOTH, ELION, IAH, TETRAGRAMMATON, SHADDÄI, LORD GOD MOST HIGH, I do exorcise thee and do power-

---

[1] Here interpolate the name of the Spirit desired to be invocated. In some of the codices there are faint variations in the form of wording of the conjurations, but not sufficient to change the sense, e.g., "Tartarean abode" for "Tartarean seat," etc.

fully command thee, O thou spirit N., that thou dost forthwith appear unto me here before this Circle in a fair human shape, without any deformity or tortuosity. And by this ineffable name, Tetragram-maton Iehovah, do I command thee, at the which being heard the elements are overthrown, the air is shaken, the sea runneth back, the fire is quenched, the earth trembleth, and all the hosts of the celestials, terrestrials, and infernals do tremble together, and are troubled and confounded. Wherefore come thou, O Spirit N., forthwith, and with-out delay, from any or all parts of the world wherever thou mayest be, and make rational answers unto all things that I shall demand of thee. Come thou peaceably, visibly, and affably, now, and without delay, manifesting that which I shall desire. For thou art conjured by the name of the Living and True God, Helioren, wherefore fulfil thou my commands, and persist thou therein unto the end, and according unto mine interest, visibly and affably speaking unto me with a voice clear and intelligible without any ambiguity.

Repeat this conjuration as often as thou pleasest, and if the Spirit come not yet, say as followeth:

THE SECOND CONJURATION

I do invocate, conjure, and command thee, O thou Spirit N., to appear and to show thyself visibly unto me before this Circle in fair and comely shape, without any deformity or tortuosity; by the name and in the name Iah and Vau, which Adam heard and spake; and by the name of God, Agla, which Lot heard and was saved with his family; and by the name Ioth, which Iacob heard from the angel wrestling with him, and was delivered from the hand of Esau his brother; and by the name Anaphaxeton[1] which Aaron heard and spake and was made wise; and by the name Zabaoth,[2] which Moses named and all the rivers were turned into blood; and by the name Asher Ehyeh Oriston, which Moses named, and all the rivers brought forth frogs, and they ascended into the houses, destroying all things; and by the name Elion, which Moses named, and there was great hail such as had not been since the beginning of the world; and by the name

---

[1] Or "Anapezeton."
[2] Or "Tzabaoth."

ADONAI, which Moses named, and there came up locusts, which appeared upon the whole land, and devoured all which the hail had left; and by the name SCHEMA AMATHIA which Ioshua called upon, and the sun stayed his course; and by the name ALPHA and OMEGA, which Daniel named, and destroyed Bel, and slew the Dragon; and in the name EMMANUEL, which the three children, Shadrach, Meshach and Abed-nego, sang in the midst of the fiery furnace, and were delivered; and by the name HAGIOS; and by the SEAL[1] OF ADONAI; and by ISCHYROS, ATHANATOS, PARACLETOS; and by O THEOS, ICTROS, ATHANATOS; and by these three secret names, AGLA, ON, TETRAGRAMMATON, do I adjure and constrain thee. And by these names, and by all the other names of the LIVING and TRUE GOD, the LORD ALMIGHTY, I do exorcise and command thee, O Spirit N., even by Him Who spake the Word and it was done, and to Whom all creatures are obedient; and by the dreadful judgments of GOD; and by the uncertain Sea of Glass, which is before the DIVINE MAJESTY, mighty and powerful; by the four beasts before the throne, having eyes before and behind; by the fire round about the throne; by the holy angels of Heaven; and by the mighty wisdom of GOD; I do potently exorcise thee, that thou appearest here before this Circle, to fulfil my will in all things which shall seem good unto me; by the Seal of BASDATHEA BALDACHIA; and by this name PRIMEUMATON, which Moses named, and the earth opened, and did swallow up Kora, Dathan, and Abiram. Wherefore thou shalt make faithful answers unto all my demands, O Spirit N., and shalt perform all my desires so far as in thine office thou art capable hereof. Wherefore, come thou, visibly, peaceably, and affably, now without delay, to manifest that which I desire, speaking with a clear and perfect voice, intelligibly, and to mine understanding.

IF HE come not yet at the rehearsal of these two first conjurations (but without doubt he will), say on as followeth; it being a constraint:

---

[1] In some "By the Seat of Adonai" or "By the Throne of Adonai." In these conjurations and elsewhere in the body of the text I have given the divine names as correctly as possible.

THE CONSTRAINT

I DO conjure thee, O thou Spirit N., by all the most glorious and effi-
cacious names of the MOST GREAT AND INCOMPREHENSIBLE LORD
GOD OF HOSTS, that thou comest quickly and without delay from all
parts and places of the earth and world wherever thou mayest be, to
make rational answers unto my demands, and that visibly and affably,
speaking with a voice intelligible unto mine understanding as aforesaid. I conjure and constrain thee, O thou Spirit N., by all the names
aforesaid; and in addition by these seven great names wherewith
Solomon the Wise bound thee and thy companions in a Vessel of Brass,
ADONAI, PREYAI or PRERAI, TETRAGRAMMATON, ANAPHAXETON or
ANEPHENETON, INESSENFATOAL or INESSENFATALL, PATHTUMON or
PATHATUMON, and ITEMON; that thou appearest here before this Circle to fulfil my will in all things that seem good unto me. And if thou
be still so disobedient, and refusest still to come, I will in the power and
by the power of the name of the SUPREME AND EVERLASTING LORD
GOD Who created both thee and me and all the world in six days, and
what is contained therein, EIE, SARAYÉ, and by the power of this name
PRIMEUMATON which commandeth the whole host of Heaven, curse
thee, and deprive thee of thine office, joy, and place, and bind thee in
the depths of the Bottomless Pit or Abyss, there to remain unto the Day
of the Last Judgment. And I will bind thee in the Eternal Fire, and into
the Lake of Flame and of Brimstone, unless thou comest quickly and
appearest here before this Circle to do my will. Therefore, come thou!
in and by the holy names ADONAI, ZABAOTH, ADONAI, AMIORAN.
Come thou! for it is ADONAI who commandest thee.

IF THOU hast come thus far, and yet he appeareth not, thou mayest be
sure that he is sent unto some other place by his King, and cannot
come; and if it be so, invocate the King as here followeth, to send him.
But if he do not come still, then thou mayest be sure that he is bound
in chains in hell, and that he is not in the custody of his King. If so, and
thou still hast a desire to call him even from thence, thou must rehearse
the general curse which is called the Spirits' Chain.

Here followeth, therefore, the Invocation of the King:[1]

---

[1] It will depend on the quarter to which the Spirit is attributed, which of the four chief
kings is to be invoked.

THE INVOCATION OF THE KING

O THOU great, powerful, and mighty King AMAIMON, who bearest rule by the power of the SUPREME GOD EL over all spirits both superior and inferior of the Infernal Orders in the Dominion of the East; I do invoke and command thee by the especial and true name of GOD; and by that God that Thou Worshippest; and by the Seal of thy creation; and by the most mighty and powerful name of GOD, IEHOVAH TETRAGRAMMATON who cast thee out of heaven with all other infernal spirits; and by all the most powerful and great names of GOD who created Heaven, and Earth, and Hell, and all things in them contained; and by their power and virtue; and by the name PRIMEUMATON who commandeth the whole host of Heaven; that thou mayest cause, enforce, and compel the Spirit N. to come unto me here before this Circle in a fair and comely shape, without harm unto me or unto any other creature, to answer truly and faithfully unto all my requests; so that I may accomplish my will and desire in knowing or obtaining any matter or thing which by office thou knowest is proper for him to perform or accomplish, through the power of GOD, EL, Who created and doth dispose of all things both celestial, aërial, terrestrial, and infernal.

AFTER thou shalt have invoked the King in this manner twice or thrice over, then conjure the spirit thou wouldest call forth by the aforesaid conjurations, rehearsing them several times together, and he will come without doubt, if not at the first or second time of rehearsing. But if he do not come, add the "Spirits' Chain" unto the end of the aforesaid conjurations, and he will be forced to come, even if he be bound in chains, for the chains must break off from him, and he will be at liberty:

THE GENERAL CURSE, CALLED THE SPIRITS' CHAIN, AGAINST ALL SPIRITS THAT REBEL

O THOU wicked and disobedient Spirit N., because thou hast rebelled, and hast not obeyed nor regarded my words which I have rehearsed; they being all glorious and incomprehensible names of the true GOD, the maker and creator of thee and of me, and of all the world; I DO by the power of these names the which no creature is able to resist, curse thee into the depths of the Bottomless Abyss, there to remain unto the Day of Doom in chains, and in fire and brimstone unquenchable, unless thou forthwith appear here before this Circle, in this triangle to do my will. And, therefore, come thou quickly and peaceably, in and by these names of God, Adonai, Zabaoth, Adonai, Amioran; come thou! come thou! for it is the King of Kings, even Adonai, who commandeth thee.

When thou shalt have rehearsed thus far, but still he cometh not, then write thou his seal on parchment and put thou it into a strong black box;[1] with brimstone, assafœtida, and such like things that bear a stinking smell; and then bind the box up round with an iron wire, and hang it upon the point of thy sword, and hold it over the fire of charcoal; and say as followeth unto the fire first, it being placed toward that quarter whence the Spirit is to come:

THE CONJURATION OF THE FIRE

I conjure thee, O fire, by him who made thee and all other creatures for good in the world, that thou torment, burn, and consume this Spirit N., for everlasting. I condemn thee, thou Spirit N., because thou art disobedient and obeyest not my commandment, nor keepest the precepts of the Lord thy God, neither wilt thou obey me nor mine invocations, having thereby called thee forth, I, who am the servant of the Most High and Imperial Lord God of Hosts, Iehovah, I who am dignified and fortified by his celestial power and permission, and yet thou comest not to answer these my propositions here made unto thee. For the which thine averseness and contempt thou art guilty of great disobedience and rebellion, and therefore shall I excommunicate thee, and destroy thy name and seal, the which I have enclosed in this box; and shall burn thee in the immortal fire and bury thee in immortal oblivion; unless thou immediately come and appear visibly and affably, friendly and courteously here unto me before this Circle, in this triangle, in a form comely and fair, and in no wise terrible, hurtful, or frightful to me or any other creature whatsoever upon the face of earth. And thou shalt make rational answers unto my requests, and perform all my desires in all things, that I shall make unto thee.

---

[1] This box should evidently be in metal or in something which does not take fire easily. (♂ [iron], who is the corruption of ☉, is best.)

AND if he come not even yet, thou shalt say as followeth:

THE GREATER CURSE [1]

Now, O thou Spirit N., since thou art still pernicious and disobedient, and wilt not appear unto me to answer unto such things as I would have desired of thee, or would have been satisfied in; I do in the name, and by the power and dignity of the Omnipresent and Immortal Lord God of Hosts IEHOVAH TETRAGRAMMATON, the only creator of Heaven, and Earth, and Hell, and all that is therein, who is the marvellous Disposer of all things both visible and invisible, curse thee, and deprive thee of all thine office, joy, and place; and I do bind thee in the depths of the Bottomless Abyss there to remain until the Day of Judgment, I say into the Lake of Fire and Brimstone which is prepared for all rebellious, disobedient, obstinate, and pernicious spirits. Let all the company of Heaven curse thee! Let the sun, moon, and all the stars curse thee! Let the LIGHT and all the hosts of Heaven curse thee into the fire unquenchable, and into the torments unspeakable. And as thy name and seal contained in this box chained and bound up, shall be choked in sulphurous stinking substances, and burned in this material fire; so in the name IEHOVAH and by the power and dignity of these three names, TETRAGRAMMATON, ANAPHAXETON, and PRIMEUMATON, I do cast thee, O thou wicked and disobedient Spirit N., into the Lake of Fire which is prepared for the damnèd and accursèd spirits, and there to remain unto the day of doom, and never more to be remembered before the face of GOD, who shall come to judge the quick, and the dead, and the world, by fire.

THEN the exorcist must put the box into the fire, and by-and-by the Spirit will come, but as soon as he is come, quench the fire that the box is in, and make a sweet perfume, and give him welcome and a kind entertainment, showing unto him the Pentacle that is at the bottom of your vesture covered with a linen cloth, saying:

---

[1] In some codices this is called "the Curse" only; but in one or two the "Spirits' Chain" is called "the Lesser Curse," and this the "Greater Curse."

THE ADDRESS UNTO THE SPIRIT
UPON HIS COMING

Behold thy confusion if thou refusest to be obedient! Behold the Pentacle of Solomon which I have brought here before thy presence! Behold the person of the exorcist in the midst of the exorcism; him who is armèd by God and without fear; him who potently invocateth thee and calleth thee forth unto appearance; even him, thy master, who is called Octinomos. Wherefore make rational answer unto my demands, and prepare to be obedient unto thy master in the name of the Lord:

BATHAL OR VATHAT RUSHING UPON ABRAC!
ABEOR COMING UPON ABERER![1]

THEN he or they will be obedient, and bid thee ask what thou wilt, for he or they be subjected by God to fulfil our desires and commands. And when he or they shall have appeared and showed himself or themselves humble and meek, then shalt thou rehearse:

THE WELCOME UNTO THE SPIRIT

WELCOME Spirit N., O most noble king[2] (or kings)! I say thou art welcome unto me, because I have called thee through Him who hast created Heaven, and Earth, and Hell, and all that is in them contained, and because also thou hast obeyed. By that same power by the which I have called thee forth, I bind thee, that thou remain affably and visibly here before this Circle (or before this Circle and in this triangle) so constant and so long as I shall have occasion for thy presence; and not to depart without my licence until thou hast duly and faithfully performed my will without any falsity.

THEN standing in the midst of the Circle, thou shalt stretch forth thine hand in a gesture of command and say:

---

[1] In the Latin, "*Bathal vel Vathat super Abrac ruens! Abeor veniens super Aberer!*" (Hence these are not names of G∴ the V∴O∴ [God the Vast One] as it would be "*ruentis,*" "*venientis.*")

[2] Or whatever his dignity may be.

"BY THE PENTACLE OF SOLOMON HAVE I CALLED THEE! GIVE UNTO ME A TRUE ANSWER!"

Then let the exorcist state his desires and requests.

And when the evocation is finished thou shalt licence the Spirit to depart thus:

THE LICENCE TO DEPART

O THOU Spirit N., because thou hast diligently answered unto my demands, and hast been very ready and willing to come at my call, I do here licence thee to depart unto thy proper place; without causing harm or danger unto man or beast. Depart, then, I say, and be thou very ready to come at my call, being duly exorcised and conjured by the sacred rites of magic. I charge thee to withdraw peaceably and quietly, and the peace of GOD be ever continued between thee and me. AMEN!

AFTER thou hast given the Spirit licence to depart, thou art not to go out of the circle until he or they be gone, and until thou shalt have made prayers and rendered thanks unto God for the great blessings He hath bestowed upon thee in granting thy desires, and delivering thee from all the malice of the enemy the devil.

Also note! Thou mayest command these spirits into the Vessel of Brass in the same manner as thou dost into the triangle, by saying: "that thou dost forthwith appear before this Circle, in this Vessel of Brass, in a fair and comely shape," etc., as hath been shown in the foregoing conjurations.

Explanation of Certain Names Used in this Book Lemegeton[1]

P[RIMUM] M[OBILE]

Eheie: Kether.	Almighty God, whose dwelling is in the highest heavens
Haioth.	The great King of heaven and all the Powers therein
Methraton.	And of all the holy hosts of Angels and Archangels
Reschith.	Hear the prayers of thy servant who putteth his whole trust in thee
Tagallalim.[2]	Let thy holy Angels command [and] assist me at this time and at all times

S[PHÆRA] Z[ODIACI]

Jehovah.	God Almighty God omnipotent hear my prayers
Hadonat.	Command thy holy Angels Above the fixed Stars
Ophamim.	To be Assisting and Aiding of thy servants
Iophiel.	That I may command all spirits of the Air fire water earth and hell
Masloth.	So that it may tend unto thy glory and man's good

---

[1] This explanation, or rather paraphrased prayer, only exists in one codex as far as my knowledge goes. The Qabalist will remark that the orthography of several of the Qabalistical names is incorrect. I give it, however, as it stands.—TRANS. {In any case it is worthless; the names mean nothing of the sort.—ED.} [This section occurs in Sloane MS. 2731; for this edition many corrections were made and lacunæ restored relying on this source, which is probably not that used by Mathers, but is generally more reliable and complete. The headings and concluding section did not appear in the 1904 first edition, and the expansions of the headings are plausible restorations.]

[2] [Mathers reads this as "Hagalgalim."]

S[PHÆRA] ♄

Jehovah.	God Almighty God omnipotent hear my prayers
Elohim.	God with us God be Always present with us
Binah.	Strengthen us and support us both now and forever
Aralim.	In these our undertakings which I do as an Instrument in thy hands
Zabbathy.[1]	Of thee the great God of Sabaoth.

S[PHÆRA] ♃

Hesel.[2]	Thou great god governor and creator of all the Planets and host of heaven
Hasmalim.[3]	Command them by thy Almighty Power
Zelez.[4]	To be now present and assisting to us thy poor servants both now and forever

S[PHÆRA] ♂

Elohim Geber.[5]	Most Almighty eternal and ever living Lord God
Seraphim.	Command thy Seraphims
Camael. Madim.	To attend on us now at this time to assist us and defend us from all perils and dangers

S[PHÆRA] ☉

Eloha.	O All mighty God be present with us both now and forever
Tetragrammaton.	And let thy Almighty power and presence ever guard and protect us at this present and forever
Raphael.	Let thy holy Angel Raphael wait upon us at this present and forever
Schemes.[6]	To assist us in this our undertakings

S[PHÆRA] ♀

Jehovah.	God Almighty God omnipotent hear my prayers
Sabaoth.	Thou great God of Sabaoth
Nezah.[7]	All seeing God
Elohim.	God be present with us and let thy presence be now and Always present with us

---

[1] [Mathers notes that Zabbathi, as his edition has it, "should be Shabbathii."]

[2] [Mathers notes that Hesel "should be Chesed," which is perhaps incorrect if this sphere pertains to Binah as the subheading indicates.]

[3] [Mathers notes that Hasmalim "should be Chashmalim."]

[4] [Mathers notes that Zelez "should be Zedeq."]

[5] [Mathers notes that Geber "should be Gibor."]

[6] [Mathers notes "or Shemesh."]

[7] [Mathers gives "Netzah, or Netzach."]

| Haniel. | Let thy holy Angel Haniel come and minister unto us at this present |

S[phæra] ☿

Elohim.	God be present with us and let thy presence be now and alway present with us
Sabaoth.	O thou great God of Sabaoth be present with us at this time and forever
Hodben.[1]	Let thy Almighty power defend us and protect us both now and forever
Michael.	Let Michael who is under thee general of thy heavenly host
Cochab.	Come and expel all evil and danger from us both now and forever

S[phæra] ☾

Sadai.	Thou great god of All Wisdom and Knowledge
Jesal.[2]	Instruct thy poor and most humble servant
Cherubim.	By thy holy Cherubim
Gabriel.	By thy holy Angel Gabriel who is the Author and Messenger of Good Tidings
Levanah.	Direct us and support us at this present and forever

THE EXPLANATION OF THE TWO TRIANGLES[3] IN THE PARCHMENT

Alpha and Omega.	Thou O great God who art the beginning and the end who was before all Eternity and ever shall be
Tetragrammaton.	Thou God of Almighty power be ever present with us to guard and protect us and let thy holy presence be now and always with us
Soluzen.	I command thou spirit of what Region soever thou art to come unto this circle
Halliza.	And Appear in human Shape
Bellatar.[4]	And speak unto us Audibly in our Mother tongue
Bellonoy.[5]	And show and discover to us all treasures that thou knowest of or that is in thy keeping and deliver it unto us quietly

[1] [Mathers notes "should be Hod simply."]
[2] [Mathers notes "should be Iesod."]
[3] Evidently meaning both the Hexagram and the Pentagram of Solomon. (*See Figures 124 and 125.*)
[4] [Mathers gives "Bellator (or Ballaton)."]
[5] [Mathers adds "or Bellony."]

Hallii Hra.[1]   And Answer us all such questions as we may
                          demand without any defect now at this time

THE EXPLANATION OF SOLOMON'S TRIANGLE

Anephezaton.[2]   Thou great God of all the Heavenly Host:
Tetragrammaton.   Thou God of almighty Power be ever present with
                          us to guard and protect us and let thy holy presence
                          be now and always with us
Primeumaton.   Thou who art the first and last let all spirits be sub-
                          ject unto us and let the spirit be bound in this Tri-
                          angle which disturbs[3] this place
Michael.   By thy holy Angel Michael until I shall discharge
                          him

North Angle.[4]   Tetragrammaton. — Thou God of Almighty Power
                          be ever present with us to guard and protect us and
                          let thy holy presence be now and always with us
Candle.   To be a light to our understandings and attend us
                          now in our undertakings and defend us from all evil
                          and danger both of soul and body

The Middle Square.   ה. Jehovah Rosh. Thou Universal God of heaven
                          and all the hosts therein and of the earth sea and air
                          and all the creatures therein
                          ו. Ioh. Thou, before thy presence all spirits both
                          infernal Airy and all others do fear and tremble let
                          them be now at this time and forever be in sub-
                          jection to me at the word of thy most holy name
                          Jehovah.

---

[1] [Mathers gives "Hallii. Hra." "Hallii" is possibly "Hally" or "Halliy," and "Hra"
    is possibly "Tira."]
[2] [Mathers gives "Anephezeton."]
[3] It is doubtful whether by "disturbs" is intended the Spirit or the triangle itself.
[4] [The descriptions of the North Angle, candles and Middle Square do not appear in
    the 1904 first edition. Sloane 2731 also adds "East Angle South and West are all
    one," probably meaning that they are the same as the North. "Angle" probably
    means subquarter, i.e. where the candles bearing the pentagrams with the name
    Tetragrammaton are placed.]

(HERE ENDETH THIS FIRST BOOK OF THE LEMEGETON, WHICH IS CALLED THE GOETIA.)

Y^{se} Conjuratiouns
of ye Booke Goetia
in ye Lemegeton

which Solomoun ye Kynge
did give unto Lemuel hys sonne,

RENDERED INTO YE MAGICALL OR ANGELIKE
LANGUAGE BY OUR ILLUSTRIOUS AND EVER-
GLORIOUS FRATER, YE WISE PERDURABO,
THAT MYGHTYE CHIEFE OF YE ROSY-CROSS
FRATERNITYE, NOW SEPULCHRED IN YE VAULT OF
YE COLLEGIUM S.S.

AND SOE MAY WE DOE ALLE!

ATTE YE BATHES OF ART

Asperges me, Domine, hyssopo, et mundabor:
Lavabis me, et super nivem dealbabor.

ATTE YE INDUYNGE OF YE HOLY VESTURES [1]

DO	KIKLE	UNAL	ZIMZ	PIR,	OL	ALDON	NANAEEL
Do -	kikalè	vaunalâ	zodimèzod	pirè,	oel	alâdonu	nanaeel
In the	mystery of	these		vestures	of the Holy Ones, I	gird up	my power

DO	ATRAAH	PIAMOL	OD	VAOAN,	DO -	LONSA	IAIDA,
do -	atârăâhe	piamoel	ōd	VôANu,	do -	elonusa	IAIDA,
in the	girdles of	righteousness	and	truth,	in the	power of	the Most High,

ANCOR:	AMACOR:	AMIDES:	THEODONIAS:	ANITOR:
Ancor:	Amacor:	Amides:	Theodonias:	Anitor:
Ancor:	Amacor:	Amides:	Theodonias:	Anitor:

CHRISTEOS	MICALZO	NANAEEL:	CHRISTEOS	APILA:
Christeos[2]	mikalazōdo	nanaeel:	christeos	apïla:
Let it be	mighty	my power:	let it	endure forever:

---

[1] [This section was extremely corrupted in the first edition. The G.D.-style vocalized Enochian, and the Enochian proper with its transliteration (both supplied for this edition), were drawn from the Golden Dawn Enochian dictionary copied by J.F.C. Fuller from the papers of Allan Bennett (Harry Ransom Humanities Research Center, University of Texas at Austin), as well as Donald Laycock's *The Complete Enochian Dictionary* (London: Askin, 1978, rpt. York Beach, ME: Weiser, 1995). Two manuscripts of interlineal Enochian Calls (one in the Fuller papers at the University of Texas, the other at Northwestern University) have also been consulted; Meric Casaubon's *A True and Faithfull Relation* (London, 1659, rpt. New York: Magickal Childe, 1992, cited herein as Casaubon) has been consulted. All sources have inaccuracies and inconsistencies, some of which are addressed in notes. The punctuation has been standardized throughout. Words have been made to align vertically in their interlineal translation, but phrases with Enochian words in a different order than their English translation are underlined in the English.]

[2] [The G.D. dictionary gives *caherisatosa*, whereas the first edition had *christeos*, one of the few instances of Crowley adopting literal Enochian transcription.]

DO - LONSA	ADONAI,	CASARM	ECRIN	OD	BUSD
do - elonusa	Adonai,	kasarèmè	e-karinu	ōd	busâdâ
in the power of	Adonai,	to whom the	praise	and	the glory

TRIAN;	LU - IPAMIS.	AMEN.
tarianu;	lu - ipamisa.	Amen.
shall be; whose	end cannot be.	Amen.

YE FYRSTE CONJOURATIOUN

OL	VAVIN	OD	ZACAM,	ILS	GAH N.:	OD
Oel	vavini	ōd	zodacamè,	Ilâsâ	gahè N.:[1]	ōd
I	invoke	and	move thee,	O thou	Spirit N.:	and

LANSH	VORSG	IAIDA,	GOHUS	PUJO	ILS,
elanusâhè	vorèsaji	IAIDA,	gohoosa	pujo	ilâsâ,
being exalted above ye in the power	of	the Most High,	I say	unto	thee,

DARBS !	DOOIAP	BERALANENSIS,	BALDACHIENSIS,	PAUMACHIA,	OD
darèbèsâ!	do-o-i-apè	Beralanensis,	Baldachiensis,	Paumachia,	ōd
Obey!	in the name	Beralanensis,	Baldachiensis,	Paumachia,	and

APOLOGIAE SEDES:	OD	MICALZO	ARTABAS,	GAH	MIR,
Apologiae Sedes:	ōd	mikalazōdo	arétabasâ,	gahè	mirè,
Apologiae Sedes:	and of the mighty		ones who govern,	spirits	[of torment],

LIACHIDAE	OD	NOQUODI	SALMAN	TELOCH:	OD
Liachidae	ōd	no-quodi	salâmanu	telocahe:	ōd
Liachidae	and	ministers of the	house	of death:	and

TABAAN	OTHIL	APOLOGIAE	DO	EM	POAMAL,	OL
tabaänu	otahila	Apologiae	do	em	Poamala,	oel
Chief Prince	of the seat	of Apologiae	in	the Ninth	Legion,[2]	I do

---

[1] (N. may = ADNI even! Since the K[ingdom] of H[eaven] suffereth violence etc.)
[2] [Lit. "palace."]

VAVIN - ILS	OD	ZACAM!	OD	LANSH	VORSG
vavini - ilâsâ[1]	ōd	zodacamè![2]	Ōd	elanusâhè	vorèsaji
invoke thee	and	by invoking thee conjure	thee!	And being exalted above ye in the power	of

IAIDA,	GOHUS	PUJO	ILS,	DARBS!	DOOIAP	TOX
IAIDA,	gohoosa	pujo	ilâsâ,	darèbèsâ!	do-o-i-apè	totza
the Most High,	I say	unto	thee,	Obey!	in the name	of him

DS	CAMLIAX	OD	AS,	CASARM	TOFGLO	TOLTORG	DARBS.
dasa	camèliatzâ	ōd	asa,	kasarèmè	tofajilo	toltoregi	darèbèsâ.
who	spake	and it	was,	to whom	all	creatures	obey.

PILAH,	OL,	DS	IAD	EOL	AZIAZOR	IAD,	DS	I	QAAL
Pilahè,	Oel,	dasa	Iadâ	e-óelâ	azodíâzōdorè	Iadâ,	dasa	i	qo-á-al
Moreover, I,		whom	God	made	in the likeness of	God,	who	is	the creator

MARB	TOX	GIGIPAH,	LRING - ILS	DOOIAP	DS
marebé	totza	jijipah,	larinuji - ilâsâ	do-o-i-apè	dasa
according to	his	living breath,	stir thee up	in the name	which

I	SALD	MICALZO	IAD,	EL,	MICALZO	OD
i	salâdâ	mikalazōdo	Iadâ,	El,	mikalazōdo	ōd
is the voice of wonder		of the mighty	God,	El,	strong	and

ADPHAHT,	ILS	GAH	N.	OD	OL	GOHUS	PUJO	ILS,
adâpehahetâ,	ilâsâ	gahè	N.	Ōd	oel	gohoosa	pujo	ilâsâ,
unspeakable,	O thou	Spirit	N.	And I		say	unto	thee,

DARBS,	DOOIAP	TOX	DS	CAMLIAX	OD	AS;	OD	DO
darèbèsâ,	do-o-i-apè	totza	dasa	camèliatzâ	ōd	asa;	ōd	do
obey,	[in the] name	of him	who	spake	and it	was;	and	in

VOMSARG,	DOOAIN	IAD.	PILAH	DOOIAP
vomèsargi,	do-ó-a-inu	Iadâ.	Pilahè	do-o-i-apè
every one of ye,	O ye names	of God.	Moreover	in the names

---

[1] [The first edition had *ta* (lit. "as") for "thee" (*ilâsâ*), probably a corruption.]

[2] [The first edition has *zodameta*, probably a corruption of *zacar* or *zodakame*, "move."]

ADONAI,	EL,	ELOHIM,	ELOHI,	EHYEH ASHER EHYEH,
Adonai,	El,	Elohim,	Elohi,	Ehyeh Asher Ehyeh,
Adonai,	El,	Elohim,	Elohi,	Ehyeh Asher Ehyeh,

ZABAOTH,	ELION,	IAH,	TETRAGRAMMATON,	SHADDAI,
Zabaoth,	Elion,	Iah,	Tetragrammaton,	Shaddai,
Zabaoth,	Elion,	Iah,	Tetragrammaton,	Shaddai,

ENAY	IAD	IAIDA,	OL	LRING - ILS;	OD	DO	UMPLIF
Enayo	Iadâ	Iaida,	oel	larinuji - ilâsâ;	ōd	do -	vamèpèlifâ
Lord	God	Most High,	I	stir thee up;	and	in	our strength

GOHUS,	DARBS!	ILS	GAH	N.	ZAMRAN	C - NOQOD
gohoosa,	darèbèsâ!	ilâsâ	gahè	N.	Zodamran	ca - no-quoda
I say	Obey!	O [thou]	Spirit	N.	Appear	unto his servants

OL	OANIO	ASPT	COMSELH	AZIAZOR	OLLOR
olé	oanio	asapeta	komselahè	azodíăzōdorè	olâlore
in a moment	before	the circle		in the likeness	of a man

OD	F ETHARZI.	OD	DOOAIP	ADPHAHT	TETRAGRAMMATON
od	fetahé-are-zodi.[1]	Ōd	do-o-a-ipè	adâpehahetâ	Tetragrammaton
and	visit me in peace.	And	in the ineffable names		Tetragrammaton

IEHEVOHE,	GOHUS,	DARBS!	SOBA	SAPAH	LANSH
Iehevohe,	gohoosa,	darèbèsâ!	soba	sapáhè	elanusâhè
Iehovah,	I say,	Obey!	whose	mighty sounds being	exalted in power

NAZ	POILP,	OZONGON[2]	CALZ	HOLDO,
nazoda	poilâpè,	ozodongon	caelzod	holādo,
the pillars are	divided, the	winds	of the firmament	groan aloud, the

PRGE	GE -	IALPON;	CAOSGA	ZACAR	DO -	GIZYAX,	OD
perèjè	je -	ialpon;	caosâga	zodăcárè	do -	gizodyazoda,	ōd
fire		burns not;	the earth	moves	in	earthquakes,	and

---

[1] [A compound of *f* (visit) and *etharzi* (peace).]

[2] [*Zongon* and its transliteration *zodongon* are given in the G.D. dictionary and Calls; the leading *o* was apparently dropped; another form is *zong*.]

ﾉﾚﾁﾆCﾚ　　　ᔭﾀCᘓﾔ　　　∩ᒷ⅂∩ﾚC　　⅃ﾁ　⅁ﾔ⅂ᒣ�61　⅃ﾁ　　ﾔﾔﾚᘓﾉ
TOFGLO　　SALMAN　　　PERIPSOL,　　OD　CAOSGI,　　OD　　FAORGT
tofajilo　salâmanu　　pè-ripesol,　　ōd　caosâji,　　ōd　　faorejita
all things of the house　of heaven,　　　and　earth,　　and the　dwelling-place of

⅃ᒷᒣ　ᘓᓄ⅂ᒣ　ﾉﾔ　ᒲ⅂ᖘᒣﾔᒥ　　⅃ﾁ　ᘓᓄ⅂ᒣ　ﾆﾚ　ᒷᒣᓄ　⅃ﾁ
ORS　　CHIS　　TA　GIZYAX,　　　　OD　CHIS　　DO - MIR,　　OD
oresâ　cahis　ta　gizodyazod,　　ōd　cahis　　do - mirè,　ōd
darkness　are　　as　earthquakes,　　and　are　　in　torment, and

⅃ᖇᘓᒲ⅃　ﾆ⅃　ᒲ⅃ᒷﾔᒥ⅃.　ᔭᒣᒣᒣ　ᒲﾔ　　ᒣCᒣ　ᒷﾔᒧ
OUCHO　　DO - CORAXO.　　NIIS,　　CA,　　ILS　GAH　N.
oucaho　do - koraxo.　　Niisa,　eka,　　ilâsâ　gahè　N.
confounded　in　thunder.　　Come forth, [therefore,] thou Spirit N.

⅃C　⅃ﾔﾆﾚᒣ　ᘓᒲᒷᒣᒣﾉᒣⅇᒣ　ﾔﾔﾚᘓﾉ　　ﾔﾔﾔﾔ　ᒣᒷᔰﾔᒷﾔᒷ　Cﾔᒣﾔﾆ
OL　OANIO:　CHRISTEOS　FAORGT　　AFFA,　IMVAMAR　LAIAD,
olé　oanio:　christeos　faorejita　afafa, imuămar　laíadâ,
in a moment:　let　　thy dwelling-place be empty, apply unto us the secrets of Truth,

⅃ﾁ　⅃ﾔⅇᐯᒣ　ᔭﾔᔭﾔᒣᒣC.　ᔭᒣᒣᒣ　ﾔ　ᒣﾉﾀᒷﾔᖘᒣ　　ᖘﾔⅇⅇᘓﾔ
OD　DARBS　NANAEEL.　NIIS,　F ETHARZI,　　ZAMRAN
od　darèbesâ　nanaeel.　Niisa,　fetahé-are-zodi,　zodamran
and　obey　my power.　Come forth, visit us in peace,　appear unto

∩ᖇᒣᒣ　⅃⅃ﾔᔭ⅃ﾔᔭ　ᖘ⅃ⅇᒣᒣ　⅃ﾔⅇᐯᒣ　ᒷᒣᒷᒣ∩ﾔᒧ　Cﾔ∩　⅃C
PUJO　OOANOAN;　ZORGE:　DARBS　GIGIPAH!　　LAP　OL
pujo　ooánoan;　zodōrèjè:　darèbesâ　jijipah!　　Lapè　oel
unto my　eyes;　　be friendly:　Obey　the living breath!　For　I

Cⅇᒣᔭᒷ　ᒣCᒣ　⅃⅃⅃ﾔᒧ　　ᒣﾔⅇ　ᔰﾔ⅃ﾔ　ﾆ⅃　ﾔᒧᒣCﾔ
LRING - ILS　DOOIAP　　IAD　VAOAN　DS　APILA,　　HELIOREN.
larinuji - ilâsâ　do-o-i-apè　Iadâ　VôANu　dasa　apĭla,　Helioren.
stir thee up　in the name of the God of Truth　who　liveth forever, Helioren.

⅃ﾔⅇᐯᒣ　ᒷᒣᒷᒣ∩ﾔᒧ　ᒲﾔ　　⅃⅃ ⅇᒣﾔⅇ　∩ᖇᒣᒣ　ᔰCᒣ　ﾉﾔ
DARBS　GIGIPAH,　CA,　　DO - MIAM　PUJO　ULS,　　TA
Darèbesâ　jijipah,　eka,　　do - miamé　pujo　vâlâsâ,　ta
Obey　the living breath, therefore, continually[1]　unto the end,　as my

ﾔᔭᒷᒣCﾔⅇ⅃　ᖘﾔⅇⅇﾔᔭ　⅃⅃ﾔᔭ⅃ﾔᔭ　　ᖘ⅃ⅇᒣᒣ　ᒷ⅃ﾔ⅃C
ANGELARD　ZAMRAN　OOANOAN:　　ZORGE:　GOHOL
anŭgelarèdâ　zodamran　ooánoan:　　zodōrèjè:　gohola
thoughts　appear　to my eyes:　therefore　be friendly:　speaking the

_____

[1] [Lit. "in continuance."]

LAIAD   DO - BIAN   OD   DO - OMP !
laíadâ   do - bianu   ōd   do - omèpè!
secrets of Truth   in   voice   and   in   understanding!

YE SECOUNDE CONJOURATIOUN

OL   VAVIN   ILS,   OD   ZACAM   ILS,   OD   LRING - ILS,
Oel   vavini   ilâsâ,   ōd   zodacamè   ilâsâ,   ōd   larinuji - ilâsâ,
I   invoke   thee,   and   move   thee,   and   stir thee up

ILS   GAH   N.:   ZAMRAN   PUJO - OOANOAN   ASPT   COMSELH
ilâsâ   gahè   N.:   zodamran   pujo - ooánoan   asapeta   komselahè
O [thou] Spirit   N.:   appear   unto my eyes   before the   circle   in the

AZIAZOR   OLLOR;   DOOAIP   OD   DOOAIP   IAH   OD   VAU,
azodíãzōdorè   olâlore;   do-o-a-ipè   ōd   do-o-a-ipè   Iah   ōd   Vau,
likeness   of a man;   in the names   and   by the name   Iah   and   Vau,

DS   ADAM   CAMLIAX: OD   DOOAIP   IAD,   AGLA,
dasa   Adam   camèliatzâ: ōd   do-o-a-ipè   Iadâ,   Agla,
which   Adam   spake: and   in the name   of God,   Agla,

DS   LOT   CAMLIAX: OD   AS   TA   OBELISONG   PUJO - TOX
dasa   Lot   camèliatzâ: ōd   asa   ta   obelisonuji   pujo - totza
which   Lot   spake: and it was   as   pleasant deliverers   unto   him

OD   TOX   SALMAN   OD   DOOAIP   IOTH   DS   IAKOB
od   totza   salâmanu: ōd   do-o-a-ipè   Ioth   dasa   Iakob
and   his   house: and   in the name   Ioth   which   Iacob

CAMLIAX,   DO - BIAN   PIR   DS   ADRPAN   TOX,
camèliatzâ,   do - bianu   pirè   dasa   adarepan   totza,
spake,   in the voice   of the Holy Ones who   cast him down,

OD   AS   TA   OBELISONG   DO   UNPH   ESAU   TOX
od   asa   ta   obelisonuji   do   vaunupeh   Esau   totza
and   was also   as   pleasant deliverers   in   the anger   of [Esau]   his

𐤃𐤅𐤅𐤉𐤅𐤁𐤌	𐤋𐤉	𐤉𐤋𐤋𐤉𐤕𐤉		𐤉𐤅	
ESIASCH:	OD	DOOAIP	ANAPHAXETON,	DS	AARON
è-si-asacah:	ōd	do-o-a-ipè	Anaphaxeton,	dasa	Aaron
brother:	and	in the name	Anaphaxeton,	which	Aaron

𐤁𐤉𐤀𐤂𐤕𐤉𐤂	𐤋𐤉	𐤉𐤅	𐤍𐤉	𐤉𐤉𐤍𐤍𐤀𐤂𐤂	𐤋𐤉	𐤉𐤋𐤋𐤉𐤕𐤉
CAMLIAX	OD	AS	TA	ANANAEL:	OD	DOOAIP
camèliatzâ	ōd	asa	ta	anánaelá:	ōd	do-o-a-ipè
spake	and	it	was	as the Secret Wisdom:	and	in the name

	𐤉𐤅		𐤁𐤉𐤀𐤂𐤕𐤉𐤂	𐤋𐤉	𐤍𐤋𐤉𐤂𐤂𐤋	𐤍𐤉𐤂𐤐𐤉𐤍
ZABAOTH	DS	MOSHEH	CAMLIAX,	OD	TOFGLO	PILZIN
Zabaoth	dasa	Mosheh	camèliatzâ,	ōd	tofajilo	pila-zodinu
Zabaoth	which	Mosheh	spake,	and	all things	of water[1]

𐤉𐤅	𐤍𐤉	𐤁𐤉𐤉𐤂𐤉	𐤋𐤉	𐤉𐤋𐤋𐤉𐤕𐤉			
AS	TA	CNILA;	OD	DOOAIP	ASHER	EHYEH	ORISTON,
asa	ta	kanîla;	ōd	do-o-a-ipè	Asher	Ehyeh	Oriston,
were	as	blood;	and	in the name	Asher	Ehyeh	Oriston,

𐤉𐤅		𐤁𐤉𐤀𐤂𐤕𐤉𐤂	𐤋𐤉	𐤍𐤋𐤉𐤂𐤂𐤋	𐤍𐤉𐤂𐤐𐤉𐤍	𐤉𐤅	𐤉𐤋𐤂𐤁𐤉𐤉
DS	MOSHEH	CAMLIAX,	OD	TOFGLO	PILZIN	AS	YOLCAM
dasa	Mosheh	camèliatzâ,	ōd	tofajilo	pila-zodinu	asa	yolacam
which	Mosheh	spake,	and	all	waters	were	bringing forth

𐤅𐤉𐤉𐤋	𐤉𐤅	𐤉𐤂𐤉𐤂	𐤉𐤅	𐤂𐤋𐤅𐤋𐤂𐤋𐤉	𐤍𐤉𐤋𐤋	𐤉𐤉𐤂𐤉𐤍
HAMI	DS	UGEG,	DS	GOHOLOR	PUJO	SALMAN,
hami	dasa	vâgéji,	dasa	goholore	pujo	salâmanu,
creatures	who	wax strong,	which	lifted up	unto the	houses,

𐤉𐤅	𐤅𐤉𐤉𐤉𐤅	𐤍𐤋𐤉𐤂𐤂𐤋	𐤋𐤉	𐤉𐤋𐤋𐤉𐤕𐤉		𐤉𐤅	
DS	QUASB	TOFGLO:	OD	DOOAIP	ELION,	DS	MOSHEH
dasa	quasâbè	tofajilo:	ōd	do-o-a-ipè	Elion,	dasa	Mosheh
which	destroy	all things:	and	in the name of	Elion,	which	Mosheh

𐤁𐤉𐤀𐤂𐤕𐤉𐤂	𐤋𐤉	𐤉𐤅	𐤉𐤂𐤂𐤉		𐤁𐤉𐤂𐤐		𐤁𐤉𐤉𐤅	𐤍𐤉
CAMLIAX,	OD	AS	ORRI		CALZ		CORS	TA
camèliatzâ,	ōd	asa	orèri		caelzod		córèsâ	ta
spake,	and	it was as	stones	from the	firmament of wrath,		such	as

---

[1] [The first edition had *zodinu* (*zin*) only; the first part of the compound was dropped. *Pilzin* means "firmament of water"; "water" is *zlida*, which the G.D. treated as a verb (to water).]

AS   GE   DO   HOMIL   ACROODZI   CAOSGO
asa   je   do   homil   acro-odzodi[1] caosâjo
was   not   in the ages   of Time the beginning   of the Earth

OD   DOOAIP   DS   MOSHEH   CAMLIAX   OD
od   do-o-a-ipè Adni, dasa Mosheh   camèliatzâ   ōd
and   in the name of Adni, which Mosheh   spake   and   there

ZAMRAN   HAMI   CAOSGO,   DS   QUASB   DS   ORRI
zodamran   hami   caosâjo, dasa quasâbè   dasa   orèri
appeared   creatures of earth,   who   destroyed   what the big stones did

GE - POILP: OD   DOOAIP   SCHEMA   AMATHIA,   DS   IOSHUA
ge - poilâpè: ōd   do-o-a-ipè   Schema   Amathia, dasa Ioshua
not   [divide]:   and   in the name   Schema   Amathia,   which Ioshua

VAVIN,   OD   ROR   PAAOX   VORS G,   VII   THIL   GIBEON
vavini, ōd   rorè   pá-aŏtza   vorèsaji, vi-i[2] tahila   Gibeon
invoked, and in the Sun   remained   over ye,   o ye hills the seats   of Gibeon

OD   DOOAIP   ALPHA   OD   OMEGA,   DS   DANIEL   CAMLIAX,
od   do-o-a-ipè   Alpha   ōd   Omega,   dasa Daniel   camèliatzâ,
and   in the names   Alpha   and Omega,   which Daniel   spake,

OD   QUASB   BEL   OD   VOVINA: OD   DOOAIP   EMMANUEL
od   quasâbè   Bel   ōd   Vouína: ōd   do-o-a-ipè   Emmanuel
and   destroyed   Bel   and the Dragon: and   in the name   Emmanuel

DS   NOR   IAD   OECRIMI   NOTHOA   IALPRG,
dasa norè   Iadâ   oé-karĭmi   notahoa   ialapereji,
which the sons of God   sang praises   in the midst of   the burning   plain,

OD   CACACOM   DO - ZILODARP: OD   DOOAIP   HAGIOS:
od   ka-cá-comè   do - zodilodarepe: ōd   do-o-a-ipè   Hagios:
and   flourished   in   conquest: and   in the name   Hagios:

---

[1] [The first edition had *ipamé* for "beginning," which is also listed in the G.D. dictionary. Laycock gives *ipam* as "is not." *Acroodzi* is used here.]

[2] [The first edition had *ili-i*, which Laycock took as a unique reading for "o ye hills." It was apparently a corruption of the G.D. dictionary listing *vi-i*, "o ye."]

OD DO - THIL ADNI: OD DO ISCHYROS, ATHANATOS,
od do - tahila Adni: ōd do Ischyros, Athanatos,
and by [in] the throne of Adni: and in Ischyros, Athanatos,

PARACLETOS: OD DO THEOS, ICTROS, ATHANATOS.
Paracletos: ōd do O Theos, Ictros, Athanatos.
Paracletos: and in O Theos, Ictros, Athanatos.

OD DO UNAL OMAOAS LAIAD AGLA, ON, TETRAGRAM-
Ōd do vaunalâ omáoas laíadâ Agla, On, Tetragram-
And in these names of secret truth Agla, On, Tetragram-

MATON, VAVIN OL OD ZACAM ILS. OD DO UNAL
maton, vavini oel ōd zodacamè ilâsâ. Ōd do vaunalâ
maton, do I invoke and move thee. And in these

OMAOAS, OD TOFGLO DS CHIS DOOAIN IAD
omáoas, ōd tofajilo dasa cahis do-ó-a-inu Iadâ
names, and all things that are the names of the God of

LAIAD DS APILA, IAIDON. OL VAVIN OD
laíadâ dasa apĭla, Ia-i-donu. Oel vavini ōd
Secret Truth who liveth forever, the All-Powerful. I invoke and

LRING ILS, ILS GAH N. NOMIG DO TOX DS GOHO
larinuji - ilâsâ, Ilâsâ gahè N. Nomiji do totza dasa goho
stir thee up, O [thou] spirit N. Even by [in] him who spake

OD AS, CASARM TOFGLO TOLTORG DARBS: OD
od asa, kasarèmè tofajilo toltoregi darèbèsâ: ōd
and it was, to whom all creatures are obedient: and

DO BALTIM OD UNPH IAD: OD DO ZIMII
do balâtimè ōd vaunupeh Iadâ: ōd do zodimĭi[1]
in the Extreme Justice and Anger of God: and by [in] the veil (?)

---

[1] [The query is in the original, which gave zodimibe for "veil"; the most likely reading is zimii, or zodimii, lit. "enter," a possible gloss for "entrance" or "veil."]

DS	I	ASPT	BUSD	IAD,	MICALZO;	OD	G	DO
dasa	i	asapeta	busâdâ	Iadâ,	mikalazōdo;	ōd	ji	do
that	is	before	the glory	of God,	mighty;	and	by[1]	[in] the

TOLTORG	GIGIPAH	ASPT	OTHIL	SOBA	OOANOAN	CHIS
toltoregi	jijipah	asapeta	otahila	soba	ooánoan	cahis
creatures of	living breath	before	the throne	whose	eyes	are

RAAS	OD	SOBOLN:	DO	PRGE	DO	IALPIRGAH	OTHIL:
ra-asa	ōd	so-bolenu:	do	perèjè	do	iala-pire-gahe	otahila:
east	and	west:	by [in]	the fire	in the	fire of just Glory	of the Throne:

DO	PIR	PERIPSOL:	OD	DO	ANANAEL	IAD:
do	pirè	pè-ripesol:	ōd	do	anánaelá	Iadâ:
by [in]	the Holy Ones of Heaven:		and by [in]	the	secret	of God:

LANSH	LRING	ILS	OL:	ZAMRAN	ASPT	UNAL
Elanusâhè	larinuji	ilâsâ	oel:	Zodamran	asapeta	vaunalâ
I, exalted in power, stir thee up:				Appear	before	this

COMSELH;	DARBS	DO	TOFGLO	DS	GOHUS:	DO
komselahè;	darèbèsâ	do	tofajilo	dasa	gohoosa:	do
circle;	obey	in	all things	that	I say:	in the

EMETGIS	BASDATHEA	BALDACHIA:	OD	DO	UNAL	DOOAIN
emetajisa	Basdathea	Baldachia:	ōd	do	vaunalâ	do-ó-a-inu
seal	Basdathea	Baldachia:	and	in	this	Name

PRIMEUMATON,	DS	MOSHEH	CAMLIAX,	OD	CAOSGI
Primeumaton,	dasa	Mosheh	camèliatzâ,	ōd	caosâji
Primeumaton,	which	Mosheh	spake,	and the earth	was

POILP,	OD	KORAH,	DATHAN,	OD	ABIRAM	LONCHO
poilâpè,	ōd	Korah,	Dathan,	ōd	Abiram	lonucaho
divided,	and	Korah,	Dathan,	and	Abiram	fell

---

[1] [Lit. "with."]

PIADPH.   CA   DARBS   DO - TOFGLO   ILS   GAH

pi-adâpehe.   Eka   darèbèsâ   do - tofajilo   ilâsâ   gahè

in the depths.   Therefore   obey   in   all things   O [thou]   spirit

N.,   DARBS   QAAN.   NIIS,   ILS   ZAMRAN

N.,   darèbèsâ   qoaän.   Niisa,   ilâsâ: zodamran

N.,   obey   thy creation.   <u>Come thou forth:</u>   appear

PUJO - OOANOAN;   F ETHARZI;   ZORGE: NIIS

pujo - ooánoan;   fetahé-are-zodi;   zodōrèjè: niisa

unto my eyes;   <u>visit us in peace;</u>   be friendly: come forth   in the

OL OANIO: DARBS   NANAEEL   GOHOL   LAIAD

olé oanio: darèbèsâ   nanaeel,   gohola   laíadâ

<u>24th of a moment:</u>   obey   my power,   speaking   the secrets of Truth

DO - BIAN   OD   DO - OMP!

do - bianu   ōd   do - omèpè!

in   voice   and   in   understanding!

YE CONSTRAYNTE

OL   LRING - ILS   ILS   GAH   N.   DO   TOFGLO   DS   CHIS

Oel   larinuji - ilâsâ   ilâsâ   gahè   N.   do   tofajilo   dasa   cahis

I   <u>stir thee up</u>   O [thou]   spirit   N.   in   all things   that   are

DOOAIN   BUSD   OD   MICALZO   IAD   DRILPA   DS

do-ó-a-inu   busâdâ   ōd   mikalazōdo   Iadâ   Darilâpa   dasa

the names   of   glory   and   power   of God   the Great One   who

I   DRILPI   OMP,   ADNI   IHVH   TZABAOTH: NIIS

i   drilâpi   omèpè,   Adni   Ihvh   Tzabaoth: niisa

is   greater   than   understanding,   Adni   Ihvh   Tzabaoth: come forth   in the

OL   OANIO: CHRISTEOS   FAORGT   AFFA;   IMVAMAR

olé   oanio: christeos   faorejita   afafa;   imuămar

<u>24th of a <u>moment</u>:</u>   let   thy   dwelling-place be empty;   apply thyself   unto the

LAIAD	OD	DARBS	NANAEEL:	ZAMRAN	PUJO -	OOANOAN,
laíadâ	ōd	darèbèsâ	nanaeel:	zodamran	pujo -	ooánoan,
secret truth	and	obey		my power:	appear	unto my eyes,

F	ETHARZI,	GOHOL	LAIAD	DO -	BIAN	OD
fetahé-are-zodi,		gohola	laíadâ	do -	bianu	ōd
visit us in peace,		speaking	the secrets of truth	in	voice	and

DO -	OMP.	OL	LRING	ILS	OD	ZACAM	ILS,	GAH	N.,
do -	omèpè.	Oel	larinuji -	ilâsâ	ōd	zodacamè	ilâsâ,	gahè	N.,
[in]	understanding.	I		stir thee up	and	move	thee, O	spirit	N.,

DO	TOFGLO	DOOAIN	DS	GOHON	I	EL:	OD	OL
do	tofajilo	do-ó-a-inu	dasa	gohonu	i	ela:[1]	ōd	oel
in	all	the names	that I	have said	[in]	[first]:	and	I

VML	UNAL	L	OD	NORZ	DOOAIN	QUIIN
vamuel	vaunalâ	elâ	ōd	nórèzod	do-ó-a-inu	quiiinu
add	these	one	and	six	names	wherein

	SOLOMON,	ENAY	ANANAEL,	AALA	AMIRAN,	GAH	VONPH,
	Solomon,	enayo	anánaelá,	aăla	amiranu,	gahè	vônupèhè,
	Solomon,	the lord	of the secret wisdom,	placed	yourselves,	spirits	of wrath,

DO -	ZIZOP	ADNI,	PREYAI,	TETRAGRAMMATON,
do -	zodizodope	Adni,	Preyai,	Tetragrammaton,
in a	vessel	Adni,	Preyai,	Tetragrammaton,

ANAPHAXETON,	INESSENFATOAL,	PATHTOMON	OD	ITEMON:
Anaphaxeton,	Inessenfatoal,	Pathtomon	ōd	Itemon:
Anaphaxeton,	Inessenfatoal,	Pathtomon	and	Itemon:

ZAMRAN	ASPT	UNAL	COMSELH;	DARBS
zodamran	asapeta	vaunalâ	komselahè;	darèbèsâ
appear	before	this	circle;	obey

---

[1] [The first edition had *eli* rather than *ela*; the sense is that of reminding the spirit of prior conjurations.]

DO	TOFGLO	NANAEEL.	OD	TA	ILS	IEH	TOX	DS
do	tofajilo	nanaeel.	Ōd	ta	ilâsâ	ieh	totza	dasa
in	all things	my power.	And	as	thou	art	he	that

GE - DARBS	OD	GE - NIIS,	OL	TRIAN,	DO - NANAEEL
je - darèbèsâ	ōd	je - niisa,	oel	tarianu,	do - nanaeel
obeys not	and	comes not,	I	shall be,	in thy power

	IAD	IAIDA	DS	APILA,	SOBA	I	QAAL	TOFGLO
O	Iadâ	Iaida	dasa	apïla,	soba	i	qo-á-al	tofajilo
O	God	Most High	that	liveth forever,	who	is	creator	of all things

DO - NORZ	BASGIM,	EIE,	SARAYE,	OD	DO - NANAEEL
do - nórèzod	basâjīm,	Eie,	Saraye,	ōd	do - nanaeel
in six	days,	Eie,	Saraye,	and	in my power

DOOIAP	PRIMEUMATON	DS	BOGPA	VORS	POAMAL
do-o-i-apè	Primeumaton	dasa	bojipa	voresa	poamala
in the name	Primeumaton	that	ruleth	over	the palaces of

PERIPSOL,	AMMA	ILS,	OD	QUASB	OTHIL,	MOZ,
pè-ripesol,	amèma	ilâsâ,	ōd	quasâbè	otahila,	mozod,
heaven,	Curse	Thee,	and	destroy	thy seat,	joy,

OD	LONSA,	OD	OL	COMMAH	ILS	PIADPH
od	elonusa,	ōd	oel	comemahe	ilâsâ	pi-adâpehe
and	power,	and	I	bind	thee	in the depth of

ABADDON,	PAAOX	CACRG	BASGIM	BALZIZRAS	SOBA
Abaddon,	pá-aŏtza	kakârèji	basâjīm	balzodizodrasâ[1]	soba
Abaddon,	to remain	until	the day	of judgment	whose

UL - IPAMIS.	OD	[OL]	COMMAH	DO	PRGE	SALBROX
ul[2] - ipamisa.	Ōd	[oel]	comemahe	do	perèjè	sálâbèrotzâ
end	cannot be.	And	I	bind	in the fire	of sulphur

---

[1] [The first edition had *zodizodarasa* rather than *balzodizodarasa* or *balzizras*.]

[2] [Both the G.D. and Crowley reversed *ul* and gave *lu* for "end." See Casaubon, p. 83, where the pronunciation *yew* is specified.]

CYNXIR	FABOAN,	OD	ZUMBI	PRGE	OD
kynutzire	faboanu,	ōd	zodumibi[1]	perèjè	ōd
mingled	with poison,	and	the seas	of fire	and

SALBROX:	NIIS,	CA,	DARBS	NANAEEL	OD	ZAMRAN
sálâbèrotzâ:	niisa,	eka,	darèbèsâ	nanaeel	ōd	zodamran
sulphur:	come forth,	therefore,	obey	my power	and	appear

ASPT	UNAL	COMSELH.	CA,	NIIS,	DOOIAP
asapeta	vaunalâ	komselahè.	Eka,	niisa,	do-o-i-apè
before	this	circle.	Therefore,	come forth,	in the name	of

PIR	ADNI,	ZABAOTH,	ADONAI,	AMIORAN.	NIIS!
pirè	Adni,	Zabaoth,	Adonai,	Amioran.	Niisa!
the Holy Ones	Adni,	Zabaoth,	Adonai,	Amioran.	Come!

LAP	ZIRDO	ADNI	DS	LRING - ILS.
lapè	zodiredo	Adni	dasa	larinuji - ilâsâ.
for	I am	Adonai	who	stir thee up.

YE POTENT INVOCATIOUN OF HYS KYNGE

ILS	DRILPA,	MICALZO	TABAAN,	AMAIMON,	DS
Ilâsâ	darilâpa,	mikalazōdo	tabaänu,	Amaimon,[2]	dasa
O thou	great,	powerful	governor,	Amaimon,	who

BOGPA	LANSH	IAIDA	EL	VORS	TOFGLO	GAH
bojipa[3]	elanusâhè	Iaida	El	voresa	tofajilo	gahè
reigneth	exalted in the power of the	only[4]	El	above	all	spirits

[1] [Laycock gives zodumebi = zumvi and cites Crowley, but gives no main entry; the word occurs in all G.D. materials as zumbi; cf. the Ninth Key.]
[2] Or Gaap, Paimon, Zodimay, as the case may be.
[3] [The G.D. misspelled this word bogra or bogira. See Casaubon, p. 83.]
[4] [Lit., "most high."]

ꓒꓕ	ꓚꓨꓙꓒꓨꟾꟷ	Ɛꓚꓮꓚ	(Ⴎꓚⴎꓚꟶꓭ	ꓕⴎ∨ꓨꓚꟶ	ꓚꓠꓐꓚꓚ)	ꓕꓚ
DO	LONDOH	RAAS	(BABAGE,	SOBOLN,	LUCAL),	OL
do	elonudohe	Ra-asa	(Babáje,	So-bolenu,	Lucalâ),	oel
[in]	[the kingdom of the]	East	(South,	West,	North),	I

ꓯꓨꓯꟷꓚ	ꓕꓚ	ꟼꓨꓐꓨꓰ	ꟾꓚꟷ	ꓚꓹꓹꓨꟷꟷ	ꓯꓨꓹꓚꟷ	Ɛꓯꓚ
VAVIN	OD	ZACAM	ILS	DOOAIP	VAOAN	MAD,
vavini	ōd	zodacamè	ilâsâ	do-o-a-ipè	VȏANu	Madâ,
invoke	and	move	thee	in the name	of the true	God,

ꓕꓚ	ꓒꓕ	Ɛꓯꓚ	ꓕⴎ∨ꓨ	ꟾꓚꟷ	ꟷꟷꟷꟷ	ꟷꓚꟷꟷ	ꓕꓚ	ꓒꓕ
OD	DO	MAD	SOBA	ILS	IEH	HOATH:	OD	DO
od	do	Madâ	soba	ilâsâ	ieh	hoatâhè:	ōd	do
and	in	God	whom	thou		worshippest:[1]	and	in	the

ꟷꓰꟷꟷꓪꟷꟷ	ꓴꓨꓨꓹ	ꓕꓚ	ꓚꓹꓹꓨꟷꟷ	Ɛꟷꓐꓨꓚꟼꓚ	Ɛꓯꓚ
EMETGIS	QAAN:	OD	DOOAIP	MICALZO	MAD,
emetajisa	qoaän:	ōd	do-o-a-ipè	mikalazōdo	Madâ,
seal	of	thy creation:	and in the	mighty names	of God,

		ꓕꓚ	ꟼꓚꓰꟷꓨꓹ	ꟾꟷꟷ
IEHEVOHE	TETRAGRAMMON,	DS	ADRPAN	ILS
Iehevohe	Tetragrammaton,	dasa	adarepan	ilâsâ
Iehevohe	Tetragrammaton,	who	cast thee down	from

ꟷꟷꓰꟷꟷꟷꓚꟷꓚ	ꟾꓚꟷ	ꓕꓚ	ꓨꓨꟷ	ꓚꓰꟷ	ꓕꓚ	ꓚꓹꓹꓨꟷꟷ	ꟷꓚꓨꓬꓚꓚ
PERIPSOL,	ILS	OD	GAH	ORS:	OD	DOOAIP	TOFGLO
pè-ripesol,	ilâsâ	ōd	gahè	oresâ:	ōd	do-o-a-ipè	tofajilo
Heaven,	thou	and the	spirits	of darkness:	and		in all the names	of the

Ɛꟷꓐꓨꓚꟼꓚ	Ɛꓯꓚ	ꓕꓚ	ꟷ	ꓴꓨꓨꓚ	ꟷꟷꓰꟷꟷꟷꓚꟷꓚ	ꓕꓚ	ꓐꓨꟷꟷꓨꟷ
MICALZO	MAD	DS	I	QAAL	PERIPSOL,	OD	CAOSGI,
mikalazōdo	Madâ	dasa	i	qo-á-al	pè-ripesol,	ōd	caosâji,
mighty	God	who	is	the creator of	Heaven,	and	earth,

ꓕꓚ	ꟼꓨꟾꓰꓨꟷ	ꓚꓰꟷ	ꓕꓚ	ꟷꓚꓨꓬꓚꓚ	ꓕꓚ	ꓒꓕ	ꓯꓚ	ꓚꓚꓹꓨꓨ
OD	FAORGT	ORS,	OD	TOFGLO;	OD	DO	UO[2]	LONSA
od	faorejita	oresâ,	ōd	tofajilo;	ōd	do	uo	elonusa
and the	dwelling	of darkness,	and	all things;	and	in	their	power

---

[1] [The first edition had *boaluahe,* a corruption for *hoatâhè* or *hoath,* "true worshipper." The *ieh* is glossed in the translation, but taken together they would give "God of whom thou art the true worshipper."]

[2] [The G.D. Calls have *uo*; this is corrupted in the G.D. dictionary to *no,* for "their"; see the Call of the 30 Æthyrs in Casaubon where it is *uo*.]

OD LUCIFTIAS; OD DOOAIP PRIMEUMATON DS BOGPA
od lukiftias; ōd do-o-a-ipè Primeumaton dasa bojipa
and brightness; and in the name Primeumaton who reigns

VORS POAMAL PERIPSOL: YOLACAM GOHUS, GAH N.,
voresa poamala pè-ripesol: Yolacam, gohoosa, gahè N.,
over the palaces of Heaven: Bring forth, I say, the spirit N.,

YOLACAM TOX OL OANIO: CHRISTEOS TOX FAORGT
Yolacam totza olé oanio: christeos totza faorejita
Bring him forth in the 24th of a moment: let his dwelling be

AFFA; CACRG F ETHARZI GOHOL LAIAD;
afafa; kakârèji fetahé-are-zodi gohola laíadâ;
empty; until he visit us in peace, speaking the secrets of truth;

CACRG DARBS NANAEEL OD TOX QAA, LONSHIN
kakârèji darèbèsâ nanaeel ōd totza qaä, elonusâhè
until he obey my power and his creation, in the power of

MAD, EL, DS I QAAL SA DS LRASD TOFGLO;
Madâ, El, dasa i qo-á-al sa dasa lârasada tofajilo;
God, El, who is the creator and [who] doth dispose of all things;

PERIPSOL, CALZ, CAOSGO, OD FAORGT ORS.
pè-ripesol, caelzod, caosâjo, ōd faorejita oresâ.
heaven, firmament, earth, and the dwelling of darkness.

YE GENERALL CURSE.
YCLEPT YE SPIRITS' CHAYNE,
AGAYNSTE ALL SPIRITS Y^T REBELLE

ILS BABALON GAH N. DS GE - DARBS, BAGLEN
Ilâsâ babalonu gahè N. dasa je - darèbèsâ, bajilenu
O thou wicked spirit N. that obeyeth not, because

OHORELA,	OD	VAVIN	OMAOAS	BUSD	OD	ADPHAHT
ohorela,	ōd	vavini	omáoas	busâdâ	ōd	adâpehahetâ
made a law,	and	invoked the	names	of the glorious	and	ineffable

MAD	VAOAN,	QAAL	TOFGLO,	OD	ILS	GE - DARBS
Madâ	VôANu,	qo-á-al	tofajilo,	ōd	ilâsâ	je - darèbèsâ
God	of Truth,	the creator of	all,	and	thou	obeyest not the

SAPAH	DS	GOHO:	CA	OL	AMMA	ILS	PIADPH
sapáhè	dasa	gohoosa:	eka	oel	amèma	ilâsâ	pi-adâpehe
mighty sounds	that	I make:[1]	therefore	I	curse	thee	in the depth of

ABADDON	PAAOX	CACRG	BASGIM	BALZIZRAS
Abaddon	pá-aŏtza	kakârèji	basâjīm	balzodizodrasâ
Abaddon	to remain	until	the day	of judgment

DO - MIR,	DO - PRGE	OD	DO	SALBROX	DS	UL IPAMIS,
do - mirè,	do - perèje	ōd	do	sálâbèrotzâ	dasa	ul ipamisa,
in torment,	in fire	and	in	sulphur	[that is]	without end,

CACRG	ILS	ZAMRAN	ASPT	COMSELH	OD
kakârèji	ilâsâ	zodamran	asapeta	komselahè	ōd
until	thou	appear	before	our will[2]	and

DARBS	NANAEEL.	NIIS,	CA,	OL OANIO,	ASPT
darèbèsâ	nanaeel.	Niisa,	eka,	olé oanio,	asapeta
obey	my power.	Come,	therefore,	in the 24th of a moment,	before the

COMSELH	DO	I-V-DU,	DOOIAP	UNAL,	OD
komselahè	do	i-v-du,[3]	do-o-i-apè	vaunalâ,	ōd
circle	in	the triangle,	in this name,	and

---

[1] [Lit. "say."]

[2] [Lit. "circle."]

[3] [This was i-be-da in the first edition, and apparently a rearrangement of du-i-be (as misspelt in the G.D. material), meaning "third angle." Crowley apparently derived "triangle" by rearrangement. See Casaubon, where it is spelt duiv, the basis for the spelling given above.]

DOOIAP — MAD, ADNI, TZABAAOTH, ADONAI, AMIORAN.
do-o-i-apè — Madâ, Adni, Tzabaoth, Adonai, Amioran.
by this name — of God, Adni, Tzabaoth, Adonai, Amioran.

NIIS! NIIS! LAP ENAY ENAY, ADONAI, DS
Niisa! Niisa! lapè Enayo Enayo, Adonai, dasa
Come! Come! for it is the Lord of Lords, Adonai, that

LRING - ILS.
larinuji - ilâsâ.
stirreth thee up.

YE CONJOURATIOUN OF YE FYRE

OL LRING - ILS, PRGE, DO TOX DS I QAAL - ILS
Oel larinuji - ilâsâ, perèjè, do totza dasa i qo-á-al - ilâsâ
I stir thee up, O thou fire, in him who is thy creator

OD TOFGLO TOLTORG: MIR, IALPON, QUASB GAH N.
od tofajilo toltoregi: mirè, ialpon, quasâbè gahè N.
and of all creatures: Torment, burn, destroy the spirit N.

PAID SOBA UL IPAMIS: OL ADPHAHT[1] ILS DO
paid soba ul ipamis: oel adâpehahetâ[1] ilâsâ do
always whose end cannot be: I judge thee in

BALZIZRAS CA[2] DO BALTIM, ILS GAH N., BAGLEN
balzodizodrasâ eka[2] do balâtimè, ilâsâ gahè N., bajilenu
judgment [as] in extreme justice, O [thou] spirit N., because

IEH TOX DS GE - DARBS NANAEEL, OD GE - DARBS DS
ieh totza dasa je - darèbèsâ nanaeel, ōd je - darèbèsâ dasa
thou art he that obeyeth not my power, and obeyeth not that

---

[1] [The first edition had *ad peranuta*, apparently a corruption of *adâpehahetâ* or *adphaht*, lit. "unspeakable." Enochian lacks a word for "judge."]

[2] [The first edition had *sa* for "and," a corruption; *ca* or *eka* is used here as it was possibly intended and approximates the meaning; "and" is literally *od*.]

OHORELA ENAY MAD, OD GE - DARBS SAPAH

ohorela enayo Madâ, ōd je - darèbèsâ sapáhè

law which the Lord God made, and obeyeth not the Mighty Sounds

OD GIGIPAH DS OL VAVIN, DS GOHUS: NIIS, OL,

od jijipah, dasa oel vavini, dasa gohoosa: Niisa, oel,

and the Living Breath which I invoke, which I send: Come forth, I,

DS ZIRDO NOCO IAIDA TABAAN ENAY IAD

dasa zodiredo noco Iaida Tabaänu Enayo Iadâ

who am the Servant of the same Most High Governor Lord God

MICALZO, IEHOVOHE, OL DS ZIRDO LANSH

mikalazōdo, Iehovohe, oel dasa zodiredo elanusâhè

powerful, Iehovohe, I who am exalted in power

DS ZIRDO MICALZO DO TOX LONSA VORSG,

dasa zodiredo mikalazōdo do totza elonusa vorèsaji,

and am mighty in his power above ye,

ILS DS GE - NIIS DLUGA ADNA GONO IADPIL DS

ilâsâ dasa je - niisa daluga adâna gono iadâpila dasa

O thou who comest not giving obedience and faith him that liveth and [who]

HOMTOH. CA GOHUS BALZIZRAS: OL AMMA - ILS,[1]

homètohè. Eka gohoosa balzodizodrasâ: oel amèma - ilâsâ,[1]

triumpheth. Therefore I say the judgment: I curse thee,

OD QUASB DOOAIN N. OD EMETGIS N., DS

od quasâbè dooain N. ōd emetajisa N., dasa

and destroy in the name N. and the seal N., which I have

OALI DO UNAL FAORGT FABOAN, OD OL IALPON

oăli do vaunalâ faorejita faboanu, ōd oel ialpon

placed in this dwelling of poison, and I burn

---

[1] [The first edition had *ta*, meaning "as" or "together." *Ilâsâ* is given for sense.]

ILS	DO	PRGE	SOBA	UL	IPAMIS;	OD	ADRPAN	ILS
ilâsâ	do	perèjè	soba	ul	ipamisa;	ōd	adarepan	ilâsâ
thee	in	fire	whose	end	cannot be;	and I	cast thee down	unto the

PIADPH	MIR,	SOBAM	VORS	ILS	GE -	TORZUL
pi-adapehé	mirè,	sobame	voresa	ilâsâ	je -	torzoduel
seas	of torment,	out of which		thou	shalt not rise	

CACRG	NIIS	PUJO -	OOANOAN:	F ETHARZI:	ZORGE
kakârèji	niisa	pujo -	ooánoan:	fetahé-are-zodi:	zodōrèjè
until	thou come	unto my	eyes:	visit me in peace:	be friendly

C -	OL	ASPT	COMSELH,	DO	I-V-DU,
ca[1] -	ōel	asapeta	komselahè,	do	i-v-du,
[unto me]		before	the circle,	in the	△, in the

OL	OANIO,	AZIAZOR	OLLOR,	GE -	CIAOFI[2]	NORMOLAP,[3]
olé	oanio,	azodíăzōdorè	olâlore,	je -	kiâofi	norè-mo-lapè,
24th of a moment,		in the likeness of a man,		not unto the terror	of the sons [of] men,	

TOLTORG,	Q - TOFGLO	VORS	ADOIAN	CAOSGO.	DARBS
toltoregi,	q - tofajilo	voresa	adoíanu	caosâjo.	Darèbèsâ
the creatures,	or all things	on	the face	of the earth.	Obey

NANAEEL,	MARB	CORDZIZ,	DARBS	GIGIPAH,
na-e-el,	marebé	corèdazodizod,	darèbèsâ	jijipah,
my power,	like	reasoning creatures,	obey	the living breath, the

OHORELA	DS	GOHUS.
ohorela	dasa	gohoosa.
law	which I	speak.

---

[1] [The first edition has "ca-ol"; the G.D. dictionary gives *k* or *ca* as "unto," usually part of the phrase "unto his servants," but listed separately.]

[2] [The G.D. calls and dictionary had *kaosi*; see Casaubon, p. 127, for this reading.]

[3] [Laycock gives *molap* as "men," deriving it from this apparent compound, as *nor*, "sons," occurs independently. See also Casaubon, p. 109.]

YE GRETER CURSE

⅃ⳑꞆⵔⵀⳑⵔ	Ɐⵆⵔⵔ	ⴹⵔⵔⴹⵔⵔⵔⳑ	ⵔⴹⵔ	ⴱⵔⵔ	Ɐⵔⴱⴹⵔⵔ
SOLPETH	- BIEN,	MADRIIAX!	ILS	GAH	N. BAGLEN
Sol-petâhè -	bienu,	Madriiatzâ!	Ilâsâ	gahè N.	bajilenu
Hearken to me [my voice],	O ye Heavens!	O thou	spirit	N.	because

ⵔⵔⴹ	ⵔⵔⵔ	ⵔⵔ	ⴱⵔ	ⵔⵔⴹⵔⵔ	ⵔⵔ	ⵔ	Ɐⵔⵔⵔⳑⵔ	ⵔⵔ
IEH	TOX	DS	GE -	DARBS	DS	I	BABALON,	OD
ieh	totza	dasa	je -	darèbèsâ	dasa	i	babalonu,	ōd
thou art	the disobedient one				who	is	wicked,	and

ⴱⵔ	ⵔⵔⴹⴹⵔⵔ	ⴱⵔⵔⵔⳑ	ⵔⵔⵔⵔ	ⴹⵔⴹⵔ	ⴱⵔⴱⵔⵔⵔⵔ
GE -	ZAMRAN	GOHOL	LAIAD	MARB	GIGIPAH:
je -	zodamran	gohola	laíadâ	marebé	jijipah:
appearest not		speaking	the secrets of truth	according to	the living breath:

ⵔⵔ	ⵔⵔⵔⵔⴹ		ⵔⵔⵔⵔ,	ⵔⵔⵔⵔⵔⴹ	ⵔⵔⴱⵔⵔ
OL,	LANSH		OIAD,	IAIDON,	ELZAP
Oel,	elanusâhè		Oïadâ,	Ia-i-donu,	elzodape
I,	exalted in the power		of God,	the All-powerful, the	centre of the

ⴱⵔⵔⵔⵔⵔⴹ	ⴹⵔⴱⵔⵔⵔⵔ	ⴹⵔⵔ	ⵔⵔ	ⵔⵔⵔⵔⵔ		ⵔⵔ	ⵔⵔⵔⴹⵔⵔ
COMSELH,	MICALZO	MAD	DS	APILA,		UL	IPAMIS,
komselahè,	mikalazōdo	Madâ	dasa	apïla,		ul	ipamisa,
circle,	powerful	God	who	liveth [forever], whose		end	cannot be,

				ⵔ	ⵔⵔⵔⵔ	ⵔⵔⴹⵔⵔⵔⵔⵔ
IEHEVOHE	TETRAGRAMMATON,			L	QAAL	PERIPSOL,
Iehevohe	Tetragrammaton,			elâ	qo-á-al	pè-ripesol,
Iehevohe	Tetragrammaton,			the only	creator	of heaven,

ⴱⵔⵔⴱⵔⴱ	ⵔⵔ	ⵔⵔⵔⴱⴹ	ⵔⴹⵔ	ⵔⵔ	ⵔⵔⵔⴱⵔⵔ	ⵔⵔ	ⴱⴹⵔⵔ	ⵔⵔ	ⵔⵔ
CAOSGO,	OD	FAORGT	ORS,	OD	TOFGLO	DS	CHIS	DO -	UO
caosâjo,	ōd	faorejita	oresâ,	ōd	tofajilo	dasa	cahis	do -	uo
earth,	and	dwelling	of darkness,	and	all		that	is	in their

ⵔⵔⴹⵔⴹⵔ	ⵔⵔ	ⵔⴹⵔⵔⵔ	ⵔⵔ	ⵔⵔⵔⵔⵔⵔⵔ	ⵔⵔⴱⵔⵔ	ⵔⵔ	ⵔⴹⵔ
POAMAL,	DS	LRASD	DO -	ANANAEL	TOFGLO	DO -	ORS
poamala,	das	lârasada	do -	anánaelá	tofajilo	do -	oresâ
palaces,	who	disposeth	in	secret wisdom	of all things	in	darkness

ⴱⵔ	ⵔⵔ	ⵔⵔⴱⵔⵔⵔⵔⵔⵔ	ⵔⴹⵔ	ⵔⵔⵔ	ⵔⵔ	ⵔⵔⴹⵔⵔⴹ	ⵔⵔⵔ	ⵔⵔ
CA	DO -	LUCIFTIAS:	AMMA	ILS	OD	ADRPAN -	ILS,	OD
eka[1] -	do -	lukiftias:	Amèma	ilâsâ	ōd	adarepan -	ilâsâ,	ōd
[as]	in	light:	Curse	thee	and	cast thee down,		and

---

[1] [The first edition had *sa* for "and," a corruption; *ca* or *eka* is used here as it was possibly intended and approximates the meaning; "and" is literally *od*.]

QUASB	OTHIL,	MOZ,	OD LONSA,	OD	OL
quasâbè	otahila,	mozod,	ōd elonusa,	ōd	oel
destroy thy seat,		joy,	and power,	and	I

COMMAH	PIADPH	ABADDON,	PAAOX	CACRG
comemahe	pi-adâpehe	Abaddon,	pá-aŏtza	kakârèji
bind	thee in the depths	of Abaddon,	to remain	until the

BASGIM	BALZIZRAS	SOBA	UL	IPAMIS,	GOHUS,
basâjīm	zodizodrasâ	soba	ul	ipamisa,	gohoosa,
day	of judgment	whose	end	cannot be,	I say,

PUJO - ZUMBI	PRGE	OD	SALBROX,	DS	ABRAMIG
pujo - zodumebi	perèjè	ōd	sálâbèrotzâ,	dasa	abèramiji
unto the seas	of fire	and	sulphur,	which I have	prepared

PUJO - BABALON	GAH,	DS	GE - DARBS,	NOR	MADRID.
pujo - babalonu	gahè,	dasa	je - darèbèsâ,	norè	madâridâ.
for the wicked	spirits,	that	obey not,	the	sons of iniquity.

CHRISTEOS	CORMFA	PERIPSOL	AMMA	ILS !
Christeos	corèmèfa	pè-ripesol	amèma	ilâsâ!
Let the	company	of heaven	curse	thee!

CHRISTEOS	ROR,	GRAA,	TOFGLO	AOIVEAE	AMMA	ILS!
Christeos	rorè,	giraä,	tofajilo	aôivéaé	amèma	ilâsâ!
Let the	sun,	moon,	all	the stars	curse	thee!

CHRISTEOS	LUCIFTIAS	OD	TOFGLO	PIR	PERIPSOL
Christeos	lukiftias	ōd	tofajilo	pirè	pè-ripesol
Let the	light	and	all	the Holy Ones of	Heaven

AMMA	ILS,	PUJO	IALPRG	DS	APILA,	OD
amèma	ilâsâ,	pujo	ialapereji	dasa	apĭla,	ōd
curse	thee,	unto the	burning flame	that	liveth forever,	and

PUJO	MIR	ADPHAHT !
pujo	mirè	adâpehahetâ!
unto the	torment	unspeakable!

OD	NOMIG	DOOAIN	OD	EMETGIS,	DS	OALI
Ōd	nomiji	do-ó-a-inu	ōd	emetajisa,	dasa	oăli
And	even as	thy name	and	seal,	which I	have put

DO - UNAL	FAORGT	FABOAN,	TRIAN	DO - MIR	NOTHOA
do - vaunalâ	faorejita	faboanu,	tarianu	do - mirè	notahoa
in this	dwelling of	poison,	shall be	in torment	among

TOLTORG	SALBROX	OD	GROSB,	OLPIRT	DO - PRGE
toltoregi	sálâbèrotzâ	ōd	jirosâbe,	olpiret	do - perèjè
creatures	of sulphur	and	bitter sting,	burning	in fire

CAOSGO,	DOOAIP	IEHEVOHE	OD	LANSH	DO - UNAL
caosâjo,	do- o-a-ipe	Iehevohe	ōd	elanusâhè	do - vaunalâ
of earth,	in them [the name] Iehevohe	and	exalted in power in	these

DOOAIN	D	TETRAGRAMMATON,	ANAPHAXETON,	OD	PRIMEUMATON,
do-ó-a-inu dau,		Tetragrammaton,	Anaphaxeton,	ōd	Primeumaton,
three names,		Tetragrammaton,	Anaphaxeton,	and	Primeumaton,

OL	ADRPAN	ILS,	GAH	BABALON	N.	PUJO -	ZUMBI
Oel	adarepan	ilâsâ,	gahè	babalonu	N.	pujo -	zodumebi
I	cast thee down,	O	wicked spirit		N.	unto	the seas

PRGEL	OD	SALBROX,	DS	ABRAMIG	PUJO -	BABALON	GAH
perejel	ōd	sálâbèrotzâ,	dasa	aberamiji	pujo -	babalonu	gahè
of fire	and	sulphur,	which	are prepared	for the	wicked	spirits

DS	GE - DARBS,	NOR - MADRID,	PAAOX	CACRG	BASGIM
dasa	je - darèbèsâ,	norè - madarida,	pá-aŏtza	kakârèji	basâjīm
that	obey not,	the sons of iniquity,	to remain	until	the day

BALZIZRAS;	BAMS - ILS	OIAD	IEHUSOZ;	ADOIAN	OIAD
balzodizodrasâ;	bamèsâ -ilâsâ	Oïadâ	jehúsozod;	adoíanu	Oïadâ
of judgment;	let the	Mercies of God forget thee;	let the face of	God

BAMS	ADOIAN	N.	DS	IPURAN	LUCIFTIAS,	IAD
bamèsâ	adoíanu	N.	dasa	ipuranu	lukiftias,	Iadâ
forget	the face	of N.	who	will not see	light,	let God

BAMS,	GOHUS,	DS	TRIAN	PIAP	BALT	VORS	NOR
bamèsâ,	gohoosa,	dasa	tarianu	piāpè	balâtâ	voresa	norè
forget,	I say,	that	shall be	the balance of	justice	over	the sons of

GIGIPAH	OD	TELOCH	OD	CAOSGI,	DO - PRGE.
jijipah	ōd	telocahe	ōd	caosâji,	do - perèjè.
living breath	and	death	and the	world,	by fire.

YE ADDRESSE UNTO YE SPIRIT ON HYS COMING

MICMA!	OL	OUCHO	ILS	TA	IEH	TOX	DS
Micama!	Oel[1]	oucaho	ilâsâ	ta	ieh	totza	dasa
Behold!	I	confound	thee	as	thou art	he	that

GE - DARBS!	MICMA	KIKLE	EMETGIS	SOLOMON	DS	OL
je - darèbèsâ!	Micama	kikalè	emetajisa	Solomon	dasa	oel
obeys not!	Behold	the mysteries of the seal	of Solomon	which I

YOLCAM	PUJO	G - MICALZO!	MICMA	QAAL,	ELZAP
yolacam	pujo	gi - mikalazōdo!	Micama	qo-á-al,	elzodape
bring forth	unto	thy power!	Behold	the creator,	the centre of the

COMSELH	GIGIPAH;	TOX	DS	I	LANSH	MAD
komselahè	jijipah;	totza	dasa	i	elanusâhè	Madâ
circle	of	the living breath; he	that	is	exalted in the	power of God

OD	IPURAN	CIAOFI:	TOX	DS	MICALZO	VAVIN	OD
ōd	ipuranu	kiâofi:	totza	dasa	mikalazōdo	vavini	ōd
and	shall not see unto the	terror:	he	that	powerfully	invoketh	and

LRING - ILS	PUJO	OOANOAN:	TOX,	ENAY	DE	G	NETAAB,
larinuji -ilâsâ	pujo	ooánoan:	totza,	enayo	de	gi	nétáăbe,
stirreth thee up	unto	visible appearance:	he,	the lord	of	thy	governments,

---

[1] [The first edition had "O" following this word, lit. "five," but probably an error.]

⅄ⅬⅤ⅄ ⅀ⅬⅬ⅄ⅬↃ ⅂ⅎⅇ⅀

SOBA	DOOAIN	IUMD	OCTINOMOS.
soba	do-ó-a-inu	ivaŭmed	Octinomos.
whose	Name	is called	Octinomos.

ⅡⅎⅇⅤⅼ Ⅾⅎ Ↄ⅄ↃⅎⅬⅬC ⅃⅄ ⅁ⅬⅇⅡ⅍⅄⅍ ⅀ⅬⅬⅎↃ

DARBS,	CA,	NANAEEL	TA	CORDZIZ,	DOOIAP
Darèbèsâ,	eka,	nanaeel	ta	corèdazodizod,	do-o-a-ipè
Obey,	therefore,	my power	as a	reasoning creature,	in the name of the

ⅬↃⅎⅼ

ENAY:

enayo:

Lord:

Bathal vel Vathat super Abrac Ruens!
Abeor veniens super Aberer!

YE WELLCOME UNTO Yᴱ SPIRIT DYGNYTIE

OL	ZIRDO	TOX	DS	I	DORPHAL	PUJO	ILS,
Oel	zodiredo	totza	dasa	i	dorèpèhala	pujo	ilâsâ,
I	am	he	that	is	looking with gladness	upon	thee,

ILS	GAH ...		TURBS	OD	ECRIN!	DORPHAL,	GOHUS,
ilâsâ	gahè ...	N.[1]	turèbès	ōd	e-karinu![2]	dorèpèhala,	gohoosa,
O thou	spirit ...	N.	beautiful	and	praiseworthy!	with gladness,	I say,

BAGLEN	IEH	IUMD	DO	TOX	DS	I	QAAL	PERIPSOL
bajilenu	ieh	ivaŭmed	do	totza	dasa	i	qo-á-al	pè-ripesol
because	thou art	called	in	him	who	is	creator	of Heaven

OD	CAOSGO,	OD	FAORGT	ORS,	OD	TOFGLO	DS	CHIS
od	caosâjo,	ōd	faorejita	oresâ,	ōd	tofajilo	dasa	cahis
and	earth,	and the	dwelling of	darkness,	and	all things	that	are

---

[1] Knights—*pu-îmè* [*puim*, lit. "sickles"]. Prelates—*tabaänu* [*tabaan*, "governor"]. Earls—*nazodpèsadâ* [*nazpsad*, "swords"]. Kings—*rorè* [*ror*, "sun"]. Dukes—*oholora* [first ed. had *oheloka*, probably a corruption; *oholora* could be glossed as "lawmaker"]. Presidents—*balâzodarèji* [*balzarg*, "steward"]. Marquises—*giraä* [*graa*, lit. "moon"].

[2] [The first edition had *akarinu*, probably a corruption for *ecrin*, lit. "praise."]

DO   POAMAL,   OD   BAGLEN   IEH   NOCO   ADNA.   DO

do-no poamala, ōd bajilenu ieh noco adâna. Do

in their palaces, and because thou art the servant of obedience. In

UNAL   LONSA   CASARMG   DARBS   GIGIPAH,   OL

vaunalâ elonusa kasarèmèjì darèbèsâ jijipah, oel

these the power by which thou art obedient to the the living breath, I

COMMAH   ILS   PAAOX   PUJO - OOANOAN   G - MICALZO

comemahe ilâsâ, pá-aŏtza pujo - ooánoan gi - mikalazōdo

bind thee, to remain visible [un]to our eyes in power

TA   NOCO   GONO   ASPT   COMSELH   CACRG   GOHUS

ta noco gono asapeta komselahè kakârèji gohoosa

as the servant of fealty before the circle until I say

"UNIGLAG   PUJO - FAORGT"   CACRG   GIGIPAH   BIAN   ENAY

"Vânijilaji pujo - faorejita" kakârèji jijipah bianu enayo

"Descend unto thy dwelling" until the living breath of the voice of the Lord

I   MARB   OHORELA   DS   TRIAN   IDLUGAM   PUJO - ILS.

i marebé ohorela dasa tarianu idâlugamè pujo - ilâsâ.

is according to the law which shall be given unto thee.

DO - EMETGIS   ANANAEL   SOLOMONIS   IEH   IUMD!

Do - emetajisa anánaelá Solomonis ieh ivaŭmed!

By the seal of the secret wisdom of Solomon thou art called!

DARBS   SAPAH!   DARBS   GIGIPAH   BIAN   ENAY!

Darèbèsâ sapáhè! darèbèsâ jijipah bianu Enayo!

Obey the mighty sounds! obey the living breath of the voice of the Lord!

Follows ye charge.

YE LICENCE TO YE SPIRIT Y^{T} HE MAYE DEPART

ILS	GAH	N.	BAGLEN	IEH	NOCO	GONO	ADNA,
Ilâsâ	gahè	N.	bajilenu	ieh	noco	gono	adâna,
O thou	spirit	N.	because	thou art the	servant of	fealty and	obedience,

OD	BAGLEN	IEH	TOX	DS	DARBS	NANAEEL	OD
ōd	bajilenu	ieh	totza	dasa	darèbèsâ	nanaeel	ōd
and	because	thou art	he	that	obeyeth	my power	and

QAAON;	CA	GOHUS:	UNIGLAG	PUJO -	FAORGT,	DARBS
quaäon;	eka	gohoosa:	Vânijilaji	pujo -	faorejita,	darèbèsâ
thy creation;	therefore	I say:	Descend unto	thy	dwelling,	obey the

OHORELA	DS	EOL,	GE -	CIAOFI	NORMOLAP,	TOLTORG,
ohorela	dasa	e-óelâ,	je -	kiâofi	norè-mo-lapè,	toltoregi,
law	which I have	made,		without terror	to the sons of men,	creatures,

TOFGLO	VORS	ADOIAN	CAOSGO.
tofajilo	voresa	adoíanu	caosâjo.
all things	upon the	surface of the	earth.

UNIGLAG,	CA,	GOHUS,	OD	BOLP	TA	BALZARG
Vânijilaji,	eka,	gohoosa,	ōd	bolape	ta	balâzodarèji
Descend,	therefore,	I say,	and	be thou	as	stewards of

COCASB:	NIIS	PAID	OL	OANIO,	NOMIG	NOQOD	DS
cocosabe:	niisa	paid	olé	oanio,	nomiji	no-quoda	dasa
Time:	come forth [always]	in a moment,		in which	even	as servants	that

TOATAR	BIAN	ENAY;	OL	OANIO	CASARMG	OL	VAVIN
toátarè	bianu	Enayo;	olé	oanio	kasarèmèjì	oel	vavini
hearken to the	voice of the Lord;		in the moment	in which		I	invoke

ILS	OD	LRING -	ILS	OD	ZACAM	ILS	DO -	KIKLE
ilâsâ	ōd	larinuji -	ilâsâ	ōd	zodacamè	ilâsâ	do -	kikalè
thee	and	stir thee up		and	move	thee	in the	mysteries of the

ANANAEL QAAL!
anánaelá qo-á-al!
secret wisdom of the Creator!

UNIGLAG PUJO - FAORGT DO - QUASAHI: CHRISTEOS
Vânijilaji pujo - faorejita do - quasahi: christeos
Descend unto thy dwelling place in pleasure: let there be the

IEHUSOZ OIAD VORS ILS: ZORGE DO - MIAM;
jehúsozod Oïadâ voresa ilâsâ: zodōrèjè do - miamé;
mercies of God upon thee: be friendly in continuing;

SOBA MIAN TRIAN BLIOR PUJO - TOLHAM. AMEN.
soba mianu tarianu beliora pujo - tolahamè. Amen.
whose long continuance shall be comforters unto all creatures. Amen.

Appendix

TABLES OF SPIRITS
IN THE GOETIA

TABLE 1: DAY DEMONS IN ASTROLOGICAL ORDER

No.	Day Demons (Hebrew)	Day Demons (English)	Day Demons (Planet)	Rank	Magical Images	Decan	Zodiacal Sign	Zodiacal Element	777 Key Scale
1	בָּאֵל	Bael	☉	King	Cat, toad, man, or all at once	1			
2	אגרא (אגראש)	Agares (Agreas)	♀	Duke	Old man, riding a crocodile and carrying a goshawk	2	♈	△	28
3	שאואן	Vassago	♃	Prince/Prelate	Like Agares	3			
4	גמיגין (גמיגין)	Samigina (Gamigin)	☽	Marquis	Little horse or ass	1			
5	מרבס (מרבש)	Marbas	☿	President	Great Lion	2	♉	▽	16
6	ואלפר (ואלפור)	Valefor	♀	Duke	Lion with ass's head, bellowing	3			
7	אמון	Amon	☽	Marquis	(1) Wolf with serpent's tail. (2) Man with dog's teeth and raven's head	1			
8	ברבטש	Barbatos	♀	Duke	Accompanied by 4 noble kings and great troops	2	♊	△	17
9	פאימון	Paimon	☉	King	Crowned king on dromedary, accompanied by many musicians	3			

TABLE 1: DAY DEMONS IN ASTROLOGICAL ORDER

No.	Day Demons (Hebrew)	Day Demons (English)	Day Demons (Planet)	Rank	Magical Images	Decan	Zodiacal Sign	Zodiacal Element	777 Key Scale
10	באר	Buer	♉	President	Probably a centaur or archer	1			
11	גוסין	Gusion	♀	Duke	"Like a Xenopilus"	2	♋	▽	18
12	שיטרי	Sitri	♃	Prince/Prelate	Leopard's head and gryphon's wings	3			
13	בלאת	Beleth *(Bileth, Bilet)*	☉	King	Rider on pale horse, with many musicians. [Flaming and poisonous breath]	1			
14	לראג	Leraje *(Leraie, Leraikha)*	☽	Marquis	An archer in green	2	♌	△	19
15	אליגוש	Eligos	♀	Duke	A knight with a lance and banner, with a serpent	3			
16	זאפר	Zepar	♀	Duke	A soldier in red apparel and armour	1			
17	בוטיש	Botis	♂ and ☿	Earl & President	Viper (or) Human, with teeth and 2 horns, and with a sword	2	♍	▽	20
18	באתין	Bathin	♀	Duke	A strong man with a serpent's tail, on a pale horse	3			

TABLE 1: DAY DEMONS IN ASTROLOGICAL ORDER

No.	Day Demons (Hebrew)	Day Demons (English)	Day Demons (Planet)	Rank	Magical Images	Decan	Zodiacal Sign	Zodiacal Element	777 Key Scale
19	שאלוש	Sallos (*Saleos*)	♀	Duke	Soldier with ducal crown riding a crocodile	1	♎	△	22
20	פורשון	Purson	☉	King	Lion-faced man riding a bear, carrying a viper. Trumpeter with him	2			
21	מאראש (מארא)	Marax	♂ and ☿	Earl & President	Human-faced bull	3			
22	יפוס	Ipos	♂ and ♃	Earl & Prince/Prelate	Angel with lion's head, goose's feet, hare's tail	1	♏	▽	24
23	אים	Aim	♀	Duke	Man with 3 heads—a serpent's, a man's (having two stars on his brow), and a calf's. Rides on viper and bears firebrand	2			
24	נבר (נברי)	Naberius	☽	Marquis	A black crane with a sore throat—he flutters	3			
25	גלאשיא-לאבולאל (גלש-)	Glasya-Labolas	♂ and ☿	Earl & President	A dog with gryphon's wings	1	♐	△	25
26	בונה	Buné (*Bimé, Bim*)	♀	Duke	Dragon with 3 heads—a dog's, man's, and gryphon's	2			
27	רונבה (רונוה)	Ronové	♂ and ☽	Earl & Marquis	A monster (probably a dolphin)	3			

Table 1: Day Demons in Astrological Order

No.	Day Demons (Hebrew)	Day Demons (English)	Day Demons (Planet)	Rank	Magical Images	Decan	Zodiacal Sign	Zodiacal Element	777 Key Scale
28	בְּרִית	Berith (*Beale, Beal, and Bofry, Bolfry*)	♀	Duke	Gold-crowned soldier in red on a red horse. Bad breath	1			
29	אשתרות (אשתארות)	Astaroth	♀	Duke	Hurtful angel on infernal dragon [...] with a viper [breath bad]	2	♑	▽	26
30	פורנאוש (פורנואוש)	Forneus	☽	Marquis	Sea monster	3			
31	פוראש	Foras	☿	President	A strong man in human shape	1			
32	אשמדאי (אשמדי)	Asmoday (*Asmodai*)	☉	King	3 heads (bull, man, ram), snake's tail, goose's feet. Rides, with lance and banner, on a dragon	2	≈	△	15
33	גאפ (גאאפ)	Gäap	☿ and ♃	President & Prince/Prelate	Like a guide [to four] kings	3			
34	פורפור (פורפיר)	Furfur	♂	Earl	(1) Hart with fiery tail. (2) Angel	1			
35	מרכושיש (מארכושיש)	Marchosias	☽	Marquis	Wolf with gryphon's wings and serpent's tail. Breathes flames	2	♓	▽	29
36	שטולוש (סטולוש)	Stolas (*Stolos*)	♃	Prince/Prelate	Raven	3			

TABLE 2: NIGHT DEMONS IN ASTROLOGICAL ORDER

No.	Night Demons (Hebrew)	Night Demons (English)	Night Demons (Planet)	Rank	Magical Images	Decan	Zodiacal Sign	Zodiacal Element	777 Key Scale
37	פאני (פאנים)	Phenex *(Pheynix)*	☽	Marquis	Child-voiced phœnix	1			
38	האלף (מאלטהוס)	Halphas *(Malthus, Malthas)*	♂	Earl	Stock-dove with sore throat	2	♈	△	28
39	מאלף (מאלטהוס)	Malphas	☿	President	Crow with sore throat	3			
40	ראום	Räum	♂	Earl	Crow	1			
41	פוקלר (פורקלור)	Focalor *(Forcalor, Furcalor)*	♀	Duke	Man with gryphon's wings	2	♉	▽	16
42	ופאר	Vepar *(Vephar)*	♀	Duke	Mermaid	3			
43	שבנוק (סאבנוך)	Sabnock *(Savnok)*	☽	Marquis	Soldier with lion's head rides pale horse	1			
44	שץ (שאץ)	Shax *(Shaz, Shass)*	☽	Marquis	Stock-dove with sore throat	2	♊	△	17
45	וינא	Viné *(Vinea)*	☉ and ♂	King & Earl	Lion on black horse carrying viper	3			

TABLE 2: NIGHT DEMONS IN ASTROLOGICAL ORDER

No.	Night Demons (Hebrew)	Night Demons (English)	Night Demons (Planet)	Rank	Magical Images	Decan	Zodiacal Sign	Zodiacal Element	777 Key Scale
46	בִּיפרונ (ביפרונש)	Bifrons (Bifröns, Bifrovs)	♂	Earl	Monster	1			
47	אואל (וואל)	Uvall (Vual, Voval)	♀	Duke	Dromedary	2	♋	▽	18
48	האגנתי (האגנתי)	Haagenti	☿	President	Bull with gryphon's wings	3			
49	קרוסל (קרוקל)	Crocell (Crokel)	♀	Duke	Angel	1			
50	פרקס (פורקש)	Furcas	♄	Knight	Cruel ancient, with long white hair and beard, rides a pale horse, with sharp weapons	2	♌	△	19
51	בלעם (באלאם)	Balam (Balaam)	☉	King	3 heads (bull, man, ram), snake's tail, flaming eyes. Rides bear, carries goshawk	3			
52	אלוס (אלוקאס)	Alloces (Alocas)	♀	Duke	Soldier with red leonine face and flaming eyes; rides great horse	1			
53	קאמי (קאיים)	Camio (Caïm)	☿	President	(1) Thrush. (2) Man with sharp sword seemeth to answer in burning ashes or coals of fire	2	♍	▷	20
54	מורמ (מורמוס)	Murmur (Murmus, Murmux)	♀ and ♂	Duke and Earl	Warrior with ducal crown rides gryphon. Trumpeters	3			

TABLE 2: NIGHT DEMONS IN ASTROLOGICAL ORDER

No.	Night Demons (Hebrew)	Night Demons (English)	Night Demons (Planet)	Rank	Magical Images	Decan	Zodiacal Sign	Zodiacal Element	777 Key Scale
55	אורבאס (אורבש)	Orobas	♃	Prince/Prelate	Horse	1			
56	גמרי (גמרי)	Gremory (Gamori)	♀	Duke	Beautiful woman, with duchess crown tied to her waist, riding great camel	2	♎	△	22
57	ועש (Oso, Voso)	Osé	☿	President	Leopard	3			
58	אמי (אונש)	Amy (Avnas)	☿	President	Flaming fire	1			
59	אוריאש (אוריאש)	Oriax (Orias)	☽	Marquis	Lion on horse, with serpent's tail, carries in right hand two hissing serpents	2	♏	▽	24
60	בפולא (נפולא)	Vapula (Naphula)	♀	Duke	Lion with gryphon's wings	3			
61	זאגן (זאגן)	Zagan	☉ and ☿	King and President	Bull with gryphon's wings	1			
62	ואלך (ואלך)	Volac (Valak, Valu, Ualac)	☿	President	Child with angel's wings rides a two-headed dragon	2	♐	△	25
63	אנדרא (אנדראש)	Andras	☽	Marquis	Angel with raven's head. Rides black wolf, carries sharp sword	3			

TABLE 2: NIGHT DEMONS IN ASTROLOGICAL ORDER

No.	Night Demons (Hebrew)	Night Demons (English)	Night Demons (Planet)	Rank	Magical Images	Decan	Zodiacal Sign	Zodiacal Element	777 Key Scale
64	דאור (דאור האור)	Haures (Hauras, Havres, Flauros)	♀	Duke	Leopard	1			
65	אנדראלף (אנדראלפוס)	Andrealphus	☽	Marquis	Noisy peacock	2	♑	▽	26
66	כימאור (כימאיס)	Cimejes (Cimeies, Kimaris)	☽	Marquis	Warrior on a black horse	3			
67	אמדור (אמדוכיאס)	Amdusias (Amdukias)	♀	Duke	(1) Unicorn. (2) Dilatory bandmaster	1			
68	בליאל	Belial	☉	King	Two beautiful angels sitting in chariot of fire	2	♒	△	15
69	דכאראב (דכראביא)	Decarabia	☽	Marquis	A star in a pentacle	3			
70	שאר	Seere (Sear, Seir)	♃	Prince/ Prelate	Beautiful man on winged horse	1			
71	דנטאל (דאנטאליין)	Dantalion	♀	Duke	Man with many countenances, all men's and women's, carries a book in right hand	2	♓	▽	29
72	אנדרומאל (אנדרומליוס)	Andromalius	♂	Earl	Man holding great serpent	3			